WATERSIDE WALKS
in the MIDLANDS

*by members of the Birmingham Group
of the Ramblers' Association*

Edited by Peter Groves

MERIDIAN BOOKS

Published 1990 by Meridian Books
Reprinted 1992
© Meridian Books 1990

British Library Cataloguing in Publication Data
Waterside walks in the Midlands
   1. England. Midlands. Recreations : Walking
   I. Groves, Peter
   796.5109424

   ISBN 1-869922-09-3

Publishers' Note
Every care has been taken in the preparation of this book but the publishers cannot accept responsibility for any inaccuracies or for any loss, damage or inconvenience resulting from the use of the book.

Meridian Books
40 Hadzor Road
Oldbury
Warley
West Midlands
B68 9LA

Maps by Angela Saunders
Printed in Great Britain by BPCC Wheatons Ltd, Exeter.

Contents

Illustrations

Foreword

Water never fails to add interest to a walk, and in Britain we are blessed with both a unique footpath network and a wide variety of waterways.

This is particularly so in the Midlands from where waterways diverge to the North sea, the Bristol Channel, the Thames Estuary and the Irish Sea.

It was with no surprise, therefore, that Peter Groves' suggestion of a book of waterside walks was greeted with enthusiasm by the City of Birmingham Group of the Ramblers' Association.

Following the invitation for contributions a dozen or so of our members donned their thinking caps first, then their boots, and finally their quills to pen the draft of twenty-two walks comprising this commendable book, published in the group's tenth anniversary year.

We all hope that you enjoy using the book and will complete most, if not all, of the rambles. Birmingham is reputed to have more miles of canals than Venice so, as you would expect, there are several canal walks. However, there are also rivers and streams, lakes and pools all awaiting your exploration. Most are circular, and all can be completed using public transport, as Peter will testify having proven every one without a car. Distances vary from three miles to twelve miles, and all contain an element of waterside walking, and all are in the English Midlands.

So, choose your first walk, pull on those boots, and don't fall in!

Roger Gibbs
Chairman: City of Birmingham Group, The Ramblers' Association.

Using this book.

Each walk in this book is accompanied by a sketch map which will normally be adequate to enable you to follow the route. However, it is always wise to also have an Ordnance Survey map, either from the Landranger series (scale 1:50,000) or, better still, from the more detailed Pathfinder series (Scale 1:25,000). In urban areas the A-Z street maps can also be very useful. As well as providing more information on your surroundings, maps are invaluable if, for any reason, you need to curtail your walk, if you get lost or, more likely, if you wish to extend your walk. We have provided the numbers of the relevant maps in the information box at the head of each walk and also grid references for the starting and finishing points.

Always have a compass, good footwear, adequate waterproofs and, especially on the longer walks, some food and a basic first aid kit.

Transport: Most of the walks are circular and will present no problems of access to motorists. In the case of the few linear walks you should normally be able to return to your car by using public transport. For these, and for non-motorists (or those who prefer to leave their cars at home), details of relevant public transport are given in the information boxes. As the Editor has been able to prove, all the walks can be reached within a day by public transport if you are starting from Birmingham. But it is wise to always check times with the bus company or British Rail before setting out. Some appropriate telephone numbers are listed below.

We have made every effort to ensure that the descriptions of the walks and the accompanying sketch maps are accurate but this cannot be guaranteed. Also, please remember that things do change. Footpaths are sometimes diverted or become overgrown. They may be ploughed over and not reinstated by the farmer (as the law requires). Footbridges may be swept away in floods; river and canal paths may be affected by erosion. We hope that you will not encounter any such problems but, if you do, the publishers will be very pleased to have details from you.

Some useful telephone numbers:

British Rail, Birmingham 021-643 2711
Bus services (West Midlands) 021-200 2700
Bus services (Staffordshire) 0785-223344
Bus services (Derbyshire) 0332 292200

Griffins Brook to Merritts Brook
by
Margaret Hodson

This is suitable for an evening stroll. Although much of it follows surfaced paths it may be muddy in places.

MAPS: Landranger 139
Birmingham A-Z
CAR PARK: Bournville Green. (Returning on 61 bus alight at Selly Oak and walk along Oaktree Lane to Bournville.)
BUS: West Midlands 11 (Outer Circle). Alight at Bournville Green. Return on No. 61 bus.
START: Bournville (GR 812045)
FINISH: Northfield (GR 798012)
DISTANCE: 3 miles.

There are a few points of interest in Bournville Green which are worth investigating before you start the walk. Go past the church of St. Francis of Assisi to Sycamore Road, turn right and about 200 yds. ahead, on the corner of Maple Road, are two ancient buildings which have been transferred from other sites — Selly Wick Manor and Minworth Greaves. These belong to the Bournville Village Trust and are open to the public (Tues - Fri inclusive, 10 am to 5 pm. Not mid-December to mid-January). Almost opposite, in the group of shops, is a coffee lounge if you like to start your walk with some refreshment.

Now return to the main road, noting the Bell Tower with a carillon which strikes the hours and the quarters. It was the gift of George Cadbury in 1906. Regular recitals are given at 8 pm on Sunday evenings in the summer.

Cross the road and turn left, then right into Bournville Park. Follow the stream — this is the Bourn which flows through the grounds of Cadbury's and joins the Rea at Dad's Lane. It is not to be confused with the Bourn Brook which flows into the Rea at Cannon Hill.

At the other end of the park cross Oak Tree Lane to enter Valley Parkway with the stream on the right. Immediately cross the stream by a footbridge and go along a surfaced path with the stream on your left.

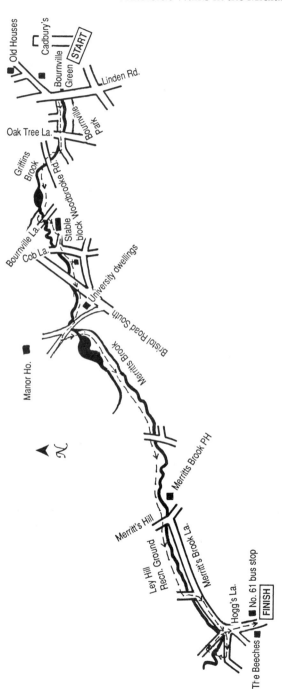

Cross Woodbrooke Road, soon crossing the stream again by a footbridge. As you approach a wooden building you will meet a large pool, a haunt of water birds, where model yachts are often sailed. Skirt the pool on the left-hand side, crossing two footbridges. Near to the second one Griffins Brook joins the Bourn.

Cross Bournville Lane to a wooded area on the left of the stream. This is a peaceful spot, within sound of the traffic along Bristol Road but screened from it by the trees. There is a well-marked path beside the stream. Towards the end of this is an old stable block, now occupied by a joinery and a building firm.

The path now becomes a drive and emerges into Cob Lane beside some attractive old cottages. Cross the lane and enter another wooded area. On the left, just after passing a footbridge on your right, you can see through the trees the dome of the Serbian Orthodox Church of St. Lazar — if you would like to visit this, walk across the grass to the car park and through the housing estate. Then return to the path.

Follow the path to Bristol Road, cross by the pedestrian crossing, turn left, walk a few yards and then go right, over the grass, into the Birmingham University housing area, keeping to the left of the stream with a row of trees and a fence on your right and the University flats on your left. Walk through the car park and turn right along the road to reach a fork. Up the hill ahead, though hidden by the trees in summer, is Manor House, formerly a home of the Cadbury family, and now, with extensive additions, a students' residence.

The old Selly Manor House in Bournville village

At the fork go left and after a few yards, just past a ramp in the road, go left through the (official) gap in the fence to the grassy area of Manor Farm Park. Skirt the little wooded area on your left and cross two small footbridges beside a very pretty tree-fringed pool. Continue along a surfaced track with the pool on the right, very soon meeting the brook again on your left.

At the far end of the pool you will see a footbridge. Make towards this but just before reaching it bear left along a flagged footpath.

Ahead you will see a rustic pavilion used for storage by the park workers, and also a toilet block — nearly always closed, unfortunately. The long gentle slope here is popular with tobogganers in winter.

The flagged path will bring you to a footbridge. Don't cross this but turn right and walk beside the stream, soon passing another footbridge. Where the stream swings left you meet a fairly well defined footpath which follows along the right hand side of the stream (though this may be difficult to spot in summer when the undergrowth is high).

The stream meanders around, passing a young wooded area on the right. Follow it to the end of the park: ignore a footbridge on the left and climb a slope to emerge onto Shenley Lane. Cross this to open ground opposite, now walking along a surfaced path which follows the course of the winding Merritt's Brook on your left.

Cross Merritt's Hill and enter Ley Hill Recreation Ground, walking beside the stream all the way. When you reach a road (Holloway) turn left, then right to walk along Merritts Brook Lane with the brook on your right. Approaching a road junction cross the grassed area on the right to meet a bridge where two lanes meet; walk up the furthest one until it bends to the left where you will see a stile and gate on your right beside a house. This leads to a footbridge which crosses Merritt's Brook as it emerges from private ground where we can no longer follow it. There is another stile and gate opposite: turn right after this to return to the first bridge. Then straight ahead, past a group of shops and opposite The Beeches, is the stop for the no. 61 bus which will take you back to the city.

Selly Oak to Woodgate Valley
by
Jenny Emerson

Despite being an urban ramble the route highlights some of the green backwaters and lanes of Birmingham. In late Spring water rats have been seen frolicking on the beds of water crowfoot in the Bourn Brook. Some fifteen species of bird have been spotted, while in late summer the berries and fruits can be as heavy as in any country lane.

MAPS: Landranger 139
Birmingham A-Z
CAR PARK: Selly Oak Park
BUSES: Outward: West Midlands 61, 62 or 63 to Selly Oak, 11 (outer circle) to Gibbins Road
Return: West Midlands 23 from Clapgate Lane or 3 from Highfield Lane
START: Selly Oak (GR 040827)
FINISH: Quinton (GR 997838)
DISTANCE : 3 miles

Our walk starts in Selly Oak at the corner of Harborne Lane and Gibbins Road, where there is a small car park. Walk through this to a wooden fence where an entrance leads onto a path which follows the course of the Dudley No. 2 Canal, disused since 1917 when the canal tunnel at Lapal collapsed. Under the bridge to the right you can still see the characteristic ridged brickwork designed to prevent horses from slipping when it was wet.

The well-made path goes left, along the old towpath, with remains of the canal visible over to your left. We shall follow the towpath to Weoley Castle.

After about half a mile the path bends right as it joins a tarmac path. After about 30 yds this tarmac path swings sharply right between two fences: go straight ahead here, still following the remains of the old canal along a good path through a nicely wooded area. Ignore a branch to the right after about 50 yds.

The path crosses a culverted stream and then soon brings us to a pedestrianised section of Bottetour Road which we cross. Continue

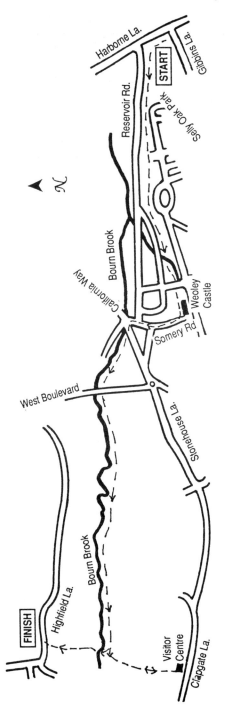

straight ahead on the path passing to the right of a school. Almost immediately the ruins of Weoley Castle can be seen on the left.

We soon meet a surfaced path by another old canal bridge. If you want to visit Weoley Castle turn left here to skirt around Weoley Castle and reach Alwold Road. The entrance to Weoley Castle is now a few yards to the left. It is open from April to October, Tuesday to Friday, 2 pm. to 5 pm. Admission is free. After visiting the castle retrace your steps to the canal bridge.

Close to Weoley Castle, on the Stonehouse Brook, there was a corn mill which dated back at least to the fifteenth century. By 1930 it had become the Mill Inn. Later all the buildings were demolished but part of the gearing was removed and may be seen in the Birmingham Museum of Science and Industry in Newhall Street.

The main route bears to the right from the canal bridge and leads along Somery Road to Stonehouse Hill. Go down Stonehouse Hill and cross California Way to enter the Woodgate Valley. The path goes beside a stream which dissects a fairly new housing development.

Cross West Boulevard carefully to enter the main section of the Woodgate Valley Country Park. This area of natural countryside and old farmland covers 450 acres and was designated as a Country Park by Birmingham

City Council in 1984. It is a fine habitat for an increasing variety of wild life. The mature hedges (some over 400 years old) are the homes of many small mammals and insects. They provide nesting sites for birds, are a source of food (in the shape of berries and nuts) for birds and mammals, and give good growing conditions for shade loving plants.

Increasing species of birds can now be seen, including pheasants, kestrels, owls, kingfishers, snipe, heron and many others that you might not expect to find so close to a large city.

Over recent years there has been an extensive programme of tree planting, adding to the variety of mature trees remaining from the time when the area was farmland.

The city has produced a series of leaflets describing the wildlife that can be seen in the park. These can be obtained from the Visitor Centre which you can visit later in this walk.

The way is well marked and there are good bridleways and footpaths to follow the meanderings of the brook. You can walk along either side of the brook or, if you wish, cross back and forth at the various weirs and bridges. The following instructions assume, however, that you are walking along the left side of the brook.

When you can see the motorway clearly ahead of you the main track swings round to the right towards a wooden bridge over the brook. There is a path going straight ahead which will take you to the Visitor Centre. If you wish to omit this continue now from the section marked below.

For the Visitor Centre follow the path forward and then take the fenced footpath to the left. This will take you directly to the Centre.

If you wish to end your walk here a number 23 bus from Clapgate Lane will take you to the city centre or to Harborne where a number 11 bus will return you to the starting point at Selly Oak.

However, if you want to continue walking retrace your steps to the point where you left the main track.

Now continue along the main track as it swings round to cross the brook by a wooden bridge. Then immediately turn right along a grassy track. Apart from the noise from the motorway this is a particularly attractive area with mature trees on the right and many young oaks on the left. You soon meet a small stream on the right which feeds into the Bourn Brook.

Go through a gap in the hedge, then bear right to cross the tiny stream into a recreation ground. Go up the right hand side of this to Highfield Lane and turn right along here for the number 3 bus. This will take you either to the city centre or to Harborne where you can catch a number 11 bus back to the starting point at Selly Oak.

3
Leasowes and Lapal
by
Margaret Hodson

A ramble along some of the small streams, tributaries of the River Stour and unnamed on the Ordnance Survey map, that meander around a delightful rural area not far from the centre of Birmingham.

MAPS: Landranger 139
Pathfinder 933 (SO88/98)
Birmingham A-Z
CAR PARK: Mucklow Hill.
BUSES: Midland Red West 131/132
West Midlands 136, 137
Alight halfway down Mucklow Hill, Halesowen at Leasowes Park.
START & FINISH: Halesowen (GR 975843)
DISTANCE: 4¾ miles

Take the path on the right-hand side of the Mucklow Hill car park alongside the now derelict section of the Dudley No. 2 Canal, where plenty of water birds can be seen. You will soon pass, at the bottom of the bank on your left, Breaches Pool which is at the end of the attractive Leasowes Valley. But this is not part of today's walk although it makes another pleasant waterside stroll.

Continue along the canal until you reach a footbridge on the right; cross this and walk along the canal to the end where it has been filled in. Emerging from here turn left onto a tarmac path and then almost immediately turn right, passing a children's play area on your left. You soon reach a main road (Manor Way); cross this carefully. The Black Horse is on your left if you are need of refreshment; otherwise turn right down the hill for about 50 yds until you reach a footpath marked 'Illey'. Climb the stile here and then another at the end of the field.

Ahead are the ruins of St Mary's Abbey, Halesowen. The Abbey was founded in 1215 on land granted by King John to the Bishop of Winchester. The monks were Premonstratensian Canons, a branch of the Augustinian order who were occupied mainly with agriculture. The Abbey became wealthy over the years, acquiring land extending south to Romsley and north to Langley. It was dissolved in 1539 by Henry VIII who gave the property to Sir John Dudley. It was originally surrounded by a moat fed by the River Stour. The ruins are now pathetically few: much more of it remained standing until the early nineteenth century.

Now aim towards the ruins; a concealed bridge will take you across the stream. Then turn left and follow the path towards a fence. Turn left alongside this.

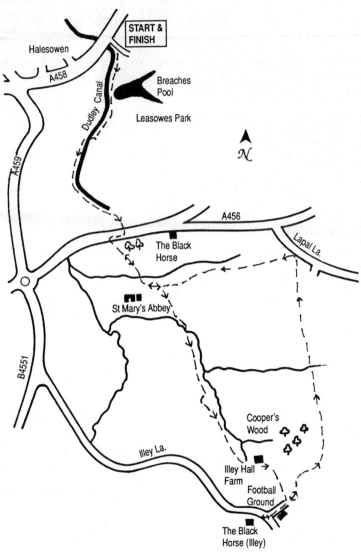

The fence ends at a stile where it is replaced by a hedge. Climb the stile and cross the field to the next stile (concealed in a dip) walking along the line of a former hedgerow, marked by an oak tree. Go over some uneven ground to a farm track and turn left along this. A stream is hidden among trees on your right. Follow the track to a crossing place, cross over, then turn left and walk beside the stream, soon passing a footbridge on the left. (If it is too muddy here walk on the higher ground along the hedge).

About 200 yds past the footbridge (where the field has now narrowed considerably) you will see, if you look up the bank to your right, a metal gate and a stile: ascend to these, climb the stile, turn left and walk along the edge of the next two fields with the stream far below you on the left.

Ruins of St Mary's Abbey

Climb the next stile to emerge on a drive. Looking back you can see the spire of Halesowen Church in the distance. Turn left towards the house, then, before you reach it turn right along the signposted path. Turn left across the end of a football field to reach two stiles in the corner. Cross the right hand stile and go right, walking along the long edge of the football field. Cross a stile, then go across a small field to another stile and onto a farm drive.

For the Black Horse (not the one that you met earlier) turn right along the drive and cross the road carefully; otherwise turn left along the drive which soon becomes a rough track. Swing round to the left, climb the stile at the end and cross the stream. Then follow the track ahead which curves round to the right into a field. Go across the field to a stile and cross this. From here the path is clearly visible leading towards a wood and a stile in the corner of the next field.

Cross the stile and walk along the edge of the wood until, about half way along the field, you reach another stile on the left. Climb this, go forward along the path, cross a stream and follow the path between hedges. Ignore a stile which you meet on your left immediately after passing through four posts.

Where the path swings round to the right look for a path towards your left where a wooden fence has been erected. Go between three posts and continue along the path until you reach another fence and three more posts. Pass between these, turn left, cross a stile, turn right and go down the hill to a stile onto Lapal Lane. There are extensive views of the Clent Hills to the left.

Don't cross the stile but take another path at right angles, still with the hedge on your right. Walk through two fields — about half-way along the second you will find a stream on your right. Enter a third field by a stile, turn right and almost immediately right again and cross a stile. (Be careful here! The ground slopes away and can be slippery.)

Now walk along the field with the hedge on your left. The stream below on your right is the one that you crossed at the beginning of your walk, and the ruins of St Mary's Abbey will soon come into view. The rectangular banks and depressions in this field are the remains of the monks' fish-ponds. Retrace your steps to the canal and Leasowes car park. Alternatively you can, if you wish, take the No. 9 bus which stops in Manor Way.

4
Brierley Hill to Cotwall End
by
Margaret Hodson

A walk along streams and pools in the Black Country, ending at the Cotwall End Nature Centre (open 9.00 to 16.30 in winter and 9.00 to 19.00 in summer).

MAPS: Landranger 139
Pathfinder: 933 (SO88/98), 912(SO89/99)
Birmingham A-Z
CAR PARK: Halesowen (then use 136 bus).
BUSES: West Midlands 136, 137. Return 558 from Sedgley to Dudley; a choice of buses from Dudley to Birmingham.
START: Brierley Hill (GR 906881)
FINISH: Cotwall End (GR 920926)
DISTANCE: 5½ miles

The 136/7 is a long winded bus which takes an hour to reach Pensnett from Birmingham on Sundays and a few minutes more on weekdays — but there is much to see on the way. Don't expect a rural ride though! It goes through Halesowen, Cradley Heath, the Merry Hill shopping complex and Brierley Hill on its way to Gornal Wood. You could make the journey less tedious by driving, or taking the No. 9 or 19 bus service to Halesowen, perhaps stopping for coffee before picking up the next 136; or by taking the train to Cradley Heath and picking up the 136 there.

Two stops after the Civic Buildings at Brierley Hill leave the bus at Brockmoor Community Centre. Continue a little way down the road and cross over towards the Brewsters pub. Go down the track beside this to the walkway beside 'Wide Waters' which is the end of the now abandoned Fens Branch of the Stourbridge Canal. Continue along the walkway which is designed to accommodate anglers — it may become rather muddy as you proceed. Reaching the end of Wide Waters the path swings left between Grove Pool (left) and Middle Pool (right). There are plenty of birds and wildfowl to be seen on both these pools and bird-watchers will want to pause and use their binoculars.

Approaching a row of houses turn right following the bank of Middle Pool: when this becomes difficult (the path disappears) ascend to

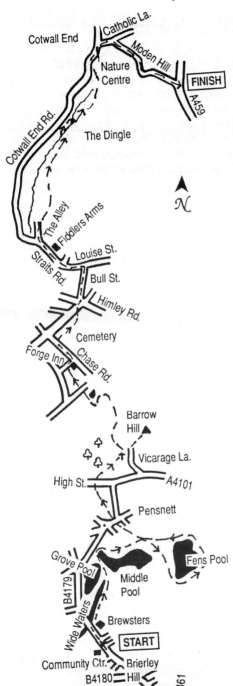

higher ground. There is a football pitch on your left and a children's playground a little further on. Passing on the left of the playground you meet the track of the old Pensnett Railway. This opened in 1845 and brought Dudley coal to the old Round Oak steelworks. The railway closed in 1966 and has been converted into a pedestrian walkway by Dudley Corporation. The site of the steelworks is now occupied by the Merry Hill shopping centre.

Turn right along the walkway making for the low brick building that you can see ahead of you. From here the track runs between Middle Pool and Fens Pool. These two pools were constructed in the early nineteenth century as feeders for the Stourbridge Canal: on a 200 year old map Grove Pool only is shown in a marshy area known as The Fens, once part of Pensnett Chase, an ancient hunting ground.

Follow the railway track until you pass between six metal posts at the far end, then a few yards further on turn left and continue round Fens Pool — there is a choice of a higher or lower path. The footpaths tend to disappear about three quarters of the way round — and The Fens lives up to its name! — but follow the general direction. Go all the way round the pool and return to the playground. Rejoin the railway track, going to the side of a gate onto this. The track is now fenced on both sides.

Proceed forward, crossing a minor road, until you arrive at a tunnel under Pensnett High Street. On emerging from the tunnel ascend the steps to your right. A few feet ahead is a narrow surfaced path leading to the attractive Pensnett churchyard — the church is almost hidden behind the trees on its high bank. Follow the path and enter the churchyard through an iron gate, then go up towards the church, passing it on your left, and emerge through the gateway at the other end. Cross the lane diagonally to your left, entering a field through a gate. Climb up the field towards the slightly crooked cross beside a trig point at the summit. The cross was erected by a former vicar one Eastertide.

You are now on Barrow Hill — not, as the name might suggest, an ancient burial mound but a solid rocky outcrop that contains the remnants of old quarries. There are extensive views from the summit — Himley Park to the north-west, Sedgley to the north, and the spire of Dudley Top Church to the north-east. Dudley Castle is hidden behind a hill and, to the south-east, Netherton Church behind two metal chimneys. You will see signs of former quarrying on the far side of the hill.

Leave the field by the same gate and re-enter the churchyard. Walk along the right-hand side of the church and swing round, keeping a low wall on your right. At the end of the wall you will reach an old gateway. Go through this onto a path through the woods. There are several interconnecting paths here: keep heading north until you enter a clearing. Here you swing round to the right passing two concrete pillars and an old quarry on your right. Continue until the path forks, taking the left-hand one which is now a well marked track between hedges. At the end turn sharply left to enter a small group of trees with a ditch on your right. Go into the field ahead: to the right is a small tree-lined pool. Go towards this in a wide arc to avoid boggy ground. Passing the pool cross the field to a gap in the hedge and rejoin the railway track. Turn right through a cylindrical tunnel and continue to a high footbridge which crosses the track.

Underneath the footbridge take the flight of steps on the right to a rough track (Forge Lane) leading, by the side of The Forge pub, into Chase Road. Turn left, passing Gornal Wood Cemetery and Crematorium on your right. Next to the cemetery is a recreation ground: cross this diagonally to the far left corner. At the end there is a gulley between houses: go through here, turn right at the top, cross Himley Road and proceed up Bull Street to the centre of Gornal Wood, arriving at the junction of Abbey Road and Louise Street. To your right is the bus station and toilets (this is the terminus for the 136/7 and for

Dudley and Wolverhampton buses). To your left is Louise Street with shops and a café. There are several pubs in Gornal Wood.

Turn left into Louise Street and continue into Straits Road. Going downhill you will soon pass on your right the Fiddlers Arms (restaurant and bar snacks during the week; restaurant only on Sundays). A little further down Straits Road take the cul-de-sac, 'The Alley', leading to a well marked path which swings right to cross a wooden footbridge. Follow the path, keeping to the left when it forks, to the wooded area ahead. Cross over the path in front of you to a well trodden track through the grass to Cotwall End Valley (marked on maps as 'The Dingle'). Descend to the stream by a flight of steps and follow it as it winds through the valley. Where a wider path crosses in front of you transfer to the opposite bank by a footbridge, go through the lower car park and ascend an embankment at the other end of the car park. The track winds round, crosses the stream, and you are soon once more walking on the right-hand bank.

The footpath ends in a long flight of steps which winds up to the right beside a seat. At the top turn left climbing a stile at the other end. On your right is the stone wall enclosing Cotwall End Nature Centre which you enter by an iron gate a little further round the wall. (If the centre is closed just carry on walking along the road until you meet the main entrance to the centre.)

Walk along the central avenue, turning right when you reach an open grassy area, then walk beside the pools which are the home of various wild fowl. Ahead and to the left are a series of pens and paddocks housing wild and domestic animals and birds — even a badger who comes out during the day, and some beautiful owls. Over to your left are the café, shop and toilets and a children's play area. A map of the area is available from the shop.

Leave Cotwall End through the main car park into Catholic Lane and take Moden Hill, a few yards up to your right. This leafy lane, first descending, then ascending steeply, soon gives superb views of distant Shropshire to the west. At the top of Moden Hill cross the road diagonally to your left for the 558 bus stop to Dudley.

5
The Netherton Tunnel and the Rowley Hills
by
Roger Gibbs

This walk explores some of the green hills of the Black Country and then takes you through the 1⅔ miles of the Netherton canal tunnel.
A torch and waterproof boots are strongly recommended for this walk.

MAPS: Landranger 139
Birmingham A-Z
CAR PARK: Warrens Hall Park, adjacent to the B4171 Blackheath — Dudley road (within easy reach of Junction 2 of the M5).
BUSES: West Midlands 140 (Birmingham-Dudley) passes Warrens Hall Park.
START & FINISH: Warrens Hall Park, Dudley (GR 956887)
DISTANCE: 9½ miles

From the car parking area or the bus stop at Warrens Hall Park (one stop past the Royal Oak public house) walk along the B4171 towards Dudley (north-westerly). Note the disused works railway embankment behind you and, a short distance along on the left, the first of the mesh covered circular brick ventilation shaft turrets. These are good indicators for the line of the Netherton Tunnel — before long you will be at the lower end of them!

In less than five minutes turn right up a track almost opposite Banklands Road and marked by a Public Footpath sign. The track climbs Rough Hill (not named on the Ordnance Survey map) soon following the line of a fence and hedge on your left. Approaching the top of the first rise look out for another ventilation shaft on your left.

After passing a pool the track ascends again, reaching a gate at the top of the rise as the main track bears to the left. Our path, however, bears right and is indicated by two stiles, emerging very soon onto a metalled quarry road.

The quarry is one of a number in the region from which has been worked the renowned 'Rowley Rag', a hard-wearing local stone on which many of Britain's roads are based. Until 1989 another two such

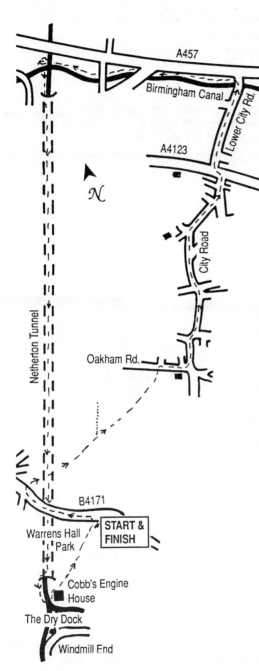

quarries, just over the hill, were divided by a narrow lane, Turners Hill. It was perhaps inevitable that the two became one, forming the largest man-made hole in Europe and destroying another unique Black Country lane in the process.

Turn left along the quarry road and then, where the road bends sharply left, take the stile on the right to cross the golf course. The path is not clearly marked, so aim for the two masts together at the top of Turner's Hill and which can be seen ahead on the skyline.

As you ascend you will soon have good views of the Clee Hills to the west.

When you reach the brow of the hill, still aiming for the two masts, you will see a modern squarely built clubhouse directly ahead. Turn left well before this, aiming to the left of a hedge and a fence. You should now have the Turner's Hill masts on your right and will have the single Darby Hill mast on your left. A fourth mast lies more distantly straight ahead.

Leave the golf course beside a bus stop onto the

Oakham Road at the top of Turner's Hill and Portway Hill. A few yards to the right is The Wheatsheaf public house.

We must now do some road walking to reach canal level and the major objective of our walk. However, it is downhill, provides some good views and should be accomplished within half an hour. From the Wheatsheaf, walk down City Road (north-east) to cross the main Birmingham-Wolverhampton road. As you descend a typical Black Country landscape lies ahead with good views of West Bromwich and Barr Beacon (the highest point for many miles around). To the right you can get some glimpses of Birmingham city centre.

Cross the main road carefully by the pedestrian crossing in front of The Huntsman public house. Maintain your direction down Lower City Road until it crosses the canal at Brades Village. Over the canal turn left down some steps to join the towpath and head north-west along the canal, now getting a more intimate view of some of the factories that you saw as you came down City Road.

Windmill End Junction and Cobb's Engine House

Shortly after the second bridge (Gilbert's Bridge) you will look down on the Netherton Tunnel Branch of the Birmingham Canal which passes under our present 'Wolverhampton level' (473 ft.). This upper canal, running from Birmingham to Wolverhampton, was built by James Brindley around 1770, keeping, as far as he could, to contours and avoiding the need to construct tunnels and cuttings. A parallel line at the 453 ft. level, and running about half a mile to the north-east, was built by Thomas Telford around 1830. This eliminated many of the twists and turns of Brindley's canal and thereby reduced the travelling distance between Birmingham and Wolverhampton by some seven miles. The Netherton Tunnel is on a branch from Telford's line. It was completed in 1858 and was the last canal tunnel to be built in Britain (apart from the 'Singing Cavern' tunnel, built within the last few years as part of the Black Country Museum complex).

Cross the bridge and turn immediately right down the slope behind the house to the lower level. Turn right onto the towpath, heading south-west into the tunnel. Now you will be glad that you remembered a torch and waterproof boots!

It will take about ¾ hr. to walk through the tunnel which is 3027 yards (2768 metres) long and perfectly straight. It was built as a by-pass to the narrow and congested Dudley Tunnel. It is 27 ft. wide, has towpaths either side, 6 ft. depth of water, 16 ft. headroom and seven ventilation shafts. It was originally lit by gas and then, later, by electricity, remains of which you can still see in the roof. All this was absolute luxury compared with the Dudley Tunnel, 9 ft. wide, no towpaths, unlit and built sixty-six years earlier. Part of the Dudley Tunnel is still open and trips are taken through it from the Black Country Museum.

The Netherton Tunnel passes through limestone, and water seeping down through this has, in a number of places, produced stalactites growing from the roof and limestone 'curtaining' on the walls. Some of this is coloured by iron which is also present in the rock. In several places streamlets of clear water produce deep puddles in the towpath.

Emerging from the tunnel you will see the remains of Cobb's engine house on your left. You are here in a former coal mining area and a pump kept the pits free of water, also providing an additional supply of water to the canal. Continue forward, passing under a bridge and then cross the canal by the fine cast iron Toll End Works bridge. You are now at Windmill End Junction.

If at this point you feel in need of refreshment you have ahead of you the Dry Dock public house which serves bar food. This contains much canal memorabilia and is particularly interesting for its bar which consists of an old canal narrow boat. To reach the pub turn right after crossing the Toll End Works bridge and cross the old Dudley No. 2 Canal by another cast iron bridge. The Dudley No. 2 originally joined the Worcester & Birmingham Canal at Selly Oak but now terminates at Halesowen. The Dry Dock, with its warning 'Beware of the Cat', is along the track which goes off slightly to the left of the canal.

Back at the Dudley No. 2 canal climb up the track back past the engine house. You are now back in Warrens Hall Park, a pleasantly landscaped open space on the site of the old pits with the remains of the tips grassed over. Continue forward up the hill to regain the car park or the B4171 for the bus.

6

Cofton Hill and the Bittell Reservoirs
by
Sylvia and Harry Hickman

A circular walk which includes part of the Lickey Hills, one of the two Bittell canal reservoirs, and part of the Birmingham & Worcester Canal.

MAPS: Landranger 139
Pathfinder: 953 (SO87/97) & 954 (SP07/17)
CAR PARK: Rose Hill car park, beside the Rose and Crown Hotel on the B4096 close to the cross roads with the B4120.
BUS: West Midlands No. 62 from Birmingham
RAILWAY STATION: Barnt Green
START & FINISH: Rednal (GR 996758) or Barnt Green (GR 006737)
DISTANCE: 8 miles.

You can start this circular walk either at Rose Hill car park on the B4096 or, if you are using public transport, at the Rednal terminus of the No. 62 bus. Alternatively you can start from Barnt Green railway station — in this case start reading from the section indicated ⇨ on page 24.

The Rose and Crown beside the car park is an old coaching inn — extra horses were stabled here to help to haul the coaches up Rose Hill.

If you are starting from here, cross the road, turn left and walk about twenty yards to reach some steps. *From the No. 62 bus terminus continue walking in the direction that you have been travelling, turn right at the roundabout and cross the road by a bus stop to reach the steps.* Climb these to the top of the ridge of Cofton Hill. Over to your left you have a good view of Cofton Reservoir and Upper Bittell Reservoir (we shall meet this later on our walk). Stay on the broad track, passing several dew ponds, relics of the time when this was pasture land. The track soon starts to descend along the side of the hill.

➡ *Continue from here if you started at Barnt Green railway station.*

The track swings left, then right: where it starts to swing left again take the smaller path on the left which leads steeply down to the B4120.

Cross the road to a footpath, signposted Cofton Church, which goes down beside some houses.

The footpath takes you over a stile into a field. Cross this field, keeping to the left hand side, to reach a tarmac path. Cross this, go over a stile and turn right by a hedge leading to a lane. Turn left along this, soon passing Cofton Church on the right where you may like to spend a few minutes looking around the churchyard. There has been a church on

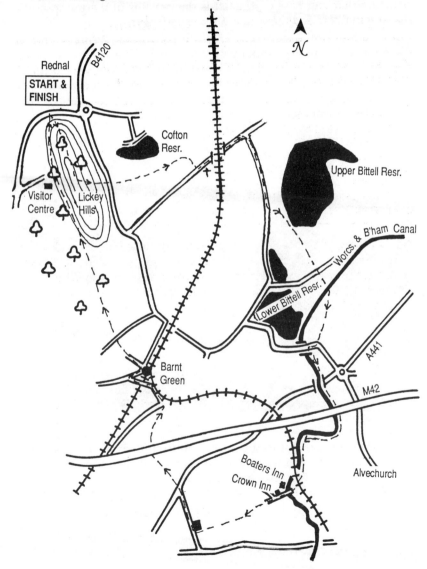

this site for about 600 years; the pinnacled bell turret, which contains two bells, dates from the fifteenth century. Close to the old timber porch there is the stone base of an ancient preaching cross.

Pass under a railway bridge and when the lane forks take the right-hand fork signposted Lower Bittell and Barnt Green Sailing and Fishing Clubs. After passing two pools take the signposted path on the left which will take you to Upper Bittell Reservoir. The great stone structure that you pass on the left is the remains of the pump-house that originally raised the water into this reservoir.

The two Bittell reservoirs were build by the Worcester and Birmingham Canal Company in the 1790s. The upper reservoir supplies water to the canal. The lower reservoir was built to compensate local mill owners for the loss of water which resulted from the construction of the canal. Both are now delightful nature reserves, popular with walkers, anglers and bird watchers.

Cofton Church

Turn right and walk along the dam. About half-way along, if you look down to the right, you will see the 'feeder' which supplies water from the dam into the Worcester and Birmingham Canal. At the end of the dam there is a Site of Special Scientific Interest, but, unfortunately, not open to the general public. Climb a stile here into a meadow and walk through this, keeping to the left-hand side. Cross another stile and continue on along what has now become a track. Cross a lane and, opposite, go past two bungalows into the farmyard of Bittell Farm. Turn

left down a farm track which will take you to a bridge over the
Birmingham and Worcester Canal.

It was, at one time, possible to gain access to the canal towpath at this
point by crossing the bridge and immediately turning left onto the
towpath. However, this is not a right of way and on our last visit we
found that it had been blocked with barbed wire. To reach the canal it
is now necessary, after crossing the bridge, to go over the stile beside a
gate on the right and then walk diagonally across the field. If the

Canal cottage and the sluices leading to the
Lower Bittell reservoir

direction of the path is obscured by crops aim for the right hand end of
the hedge which you can see across on the other side of the field
(bearing 180°). Just past the corner of the hedge cross a bridge and go
up, over a stile, onto the road. Turn right to reach a bridge (No. 65) over
the canal.

If you have time it is worth going down on the right hand side of the
bridge, turning right and walking a little way back to see the canal
cottage and the sluices which control the flow of water down to the
Lower Bittell Reservoir.

Otherwise go down the steps on the left hand side of the bridge, turn
left and walk along the towpath which soon passes under the M42. The
400 yd. stretch of canal here was rebuilt when the motorway was built
— with the canal in its original position the elevated section of the
motorway running west from Alvechurch would have needed to be

eight feet or more higher. The bed of the new canal was sealed with clay just as the original builders had done nearly 200 years ago. Go over the wooden footbridge which crosses the remnants of the old canal and regain the towpath.

Go under two bridges and then leave the towpath at bridge 61. Turn left and walk over the canal bridge and past the Crown Inn. At the end of the lane you reach a signposted footpath to Foxhill Lane. Go over the stile and follow the path up the hillside through two fields. Leave the second field near to the right hand corner and walk up another field with a fence and row of trees on your right. Go through a metal gate into a farmyard and, after passing the farmhouse on your left, turn right along Foxhill Lane. At the T-junction you will see, opposite, a stile and a signposted path to Barnt Green. Take the path, keeping to the right-hand boundary of the field and passing a coppice on the right.

Cross a stile to a footbridge over the M42 and leading into a meadow. Cross this, keeping to the left-hand edge and descending towards some houses. A stile will take you to a path alongside the houses leading to the road. Turn right here, then first left into Hewell Lane just before a railway bridge. At the T-junction turn right to reach Barnt Green railway station.

⇨   *If you are using the train, start and end your walk here.*

Opposite Barnt Green station take the footpath between an avenue of trees. Cross the lane and follow a bridle path for about a mile through the Lickey Hills, taking the right-hand fork when you reach a wooden shelter and ignoring all side paths. The path will bring you to the Lickey Hills Visitor Centre.

If you started your walk at Barnt Green station turn right onto the road here which leads to a car park. Go across the car park and then straight ahead, keeping to the left of the trees. This will bring you to a path which descends along the side of Cofton Hill. Now continue from the point marked ➡ on page 20.

If you started from the Rose Hill car park or from the bus stop cross the road and take the surfaced bridle path which runs between an old quarry and the Lickey Hills Nursing Home. This will lead you onto the B4096. Turn left along this for the Rose Hill car park, or right to retrace your steps to the terminus of the No. 62 bus.

7

Hagley and Belbroughton
by
Roger Gibbs

A circular walk below the Clent Hills, passing through some delightful North Worcestershire villages and featuring a stream-side valley walk.

MAPS: Landranger 139
Pathfinder: 953 (SO87/97) and 933 (SO88/98)
CAR PARKING: The best car parking is to be found on the A491 Hagley to Bromsgrove Road a few yards past the footpath which the walk follows. A good lay-by will be easily found at GR 928782 and is, in fact, marked on some OS maps. The script assumes that the walk is started from this point. Alternatively, some parking may be found in Hagley itself.
BUSES: Midland Red West X92, X93 to Hagley
RAILWAY STATION: Hagley
START & FINISH: A491 (cars only) (GR 928782)
or Hagley (buses or cars or trains) (GR 914808). *If you start from Hagley you should join the walk at GR 914808 as indicated by* ➡ *on page 29.*
DISTANCE: 11 miles.

Starting from the lay-by on the A491, take the footpath signposted to Belbroughton Village ½ mile and going south-west. You will find a stile in the hedge opposite the more obvious sign to Walton Pool.

Keep the hedge on your left until you reach a kissing gate, from which point the hedge has been removed. Maintain the same direction, following a line of trees across the open field to another old kissing gate, now disused and converted to a stile. Bear slightly left to pick up a footbridge. This is the first section of waterside on our walk. Intermittently we will be alongside water for much of the next four miles, and again after that.

Having crossed the footbridge over the pool, follow the clearly laid path through the woods to emerge on a lane into Belbroughton. Turn right along the lane and follow it until the T-junction, ignoring a footpath to the left. There is an attractive pool in the garden of the large house to the right — a weir brings water from it cascading down to a stream that passes under the road. Cross straight over the road at the

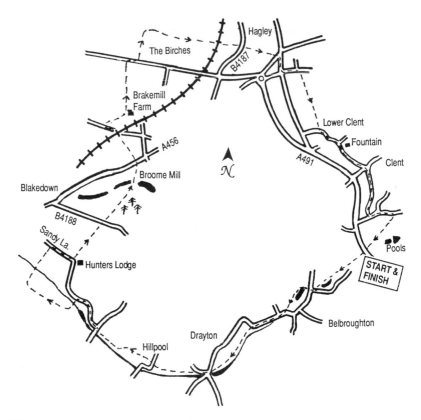

T-junction and take the marked public footpath to the left of a rather
fine looking house.

After a few yards turn left at the rear of the houses, keeping the hedge
on the left. The path is quite well marked on the ground and makes its
way through the hawthorns. Emerging by some old works, keep
straight on to pass to the back of them, with the wall immediately to
the left.

The footpath joins the road by the Queens Hotel in Drayton Road.
Turn right and, as the main road bends to the right to Blakedown and
Kidderminster (B4188), keep straight on along the lane towards
Drayton and Chaddesley Corbett.

You will notice the old pools on the left, the first of several, and just
below the pool may be seen some millstones, relics of previous industry.

After about five minutes road walking the lane turns to the right. At
this point leave the lane, taking a signed footpath on the right hand
bank of the stream. Over the stile keep the stream and pools on your

left until you come out on the road. Half-way along this stretch you will pass a footbridge. Although it is a right of way do not cross this bridge, which was used to service the works on the opposite bank of the stream. Instead, keep along the stream, crossing several stiles. The 'Trespassers will be Prosecuted' sign at Drayton Pool refers to the pool edges and need not worry us. The path is an established right of way.

Coming out onto the lane at Drayton bear left and then right at the first road junction. Ignore the footpath sign just before the junction, but take the metalled road, signposted Hillpool and Yieldingtree, for a few hundred yards until it swings off to the right. Just past a cottage called 'Otter Bank' join the footpath which goes off to the left, retaining the direction of the stream and signposted Hillpool. The way is clear, keeping the stream on the left, until Hillpool and beyond.

As you approach some farm buildings go over two stiles and down to a farm drive. An old mill is on your left. Turn right along the drive to emerge onto the lane at Hillpool. Just across the lane, to the right, is a house alongside which the footpath continues. Keep the house and its gardens on your left and continue along the line of the stream and over a footbridge crossing a disused mill-race.

Cross over a stile to gain the river-bank proper in front of a fine riverside house on the opposite bank. The path gently follows the river-bank with the disused mill-race to the right and the stream to the left. Boggy conditions underfoot will make good boots worthwhile here, at least until the path rises up to the right passing between two lines of trees, past a seat and over a stile. As the path drops down again you will see a footbridge which takes us over to the opposite side of the stream for the first time. The path climbs up the bank to the right and continues alongside the hedge at the top of the bank, the stream now running below to our right.

After negotiating a stile you may be able to spot the old mill-wheel at the side of the buildings over the stream. This is the destination of the mill-race that we met earlier.

Over another stile we are back on the road for another short stretch of road-walking. Turn right across the stream again, then first left down Sandy Lane alongside the stream, now developing into pools.

Follow the road past farm buildings, a conifer hedge, then a hawthorn hedge, for about ¼ mile to a track off to the left marked with a footpath sign. Go down the track, among the hawthorn bushes, over another disused mill-race and the main stream, keeping two old buildings on your right and passing behind the second one (an ivy covered pump-house) to turn right alongside the stream once more.

We are now at the bottom hedge of a large field with farm buildings up to the left. Leave the field at its bottom corner and continue along the bank of the water, keeping a sharp look-out for wildfowl.

The stream meanders away to the right through a small wood but soon returns to a pool. As the pool reverts to a stream again a stile will be seen by some old brickwork. Go over the stile, cross back over the stream by a wooden footbridge and climb the bank. Up the bank cross a stile and go straight across the field to another stile at the side of a tree bearing a 'No Horses' sign but indicating the footpath.

Go straight up the hill and to the right of the woods on top, then follow the track down to the lane at the end where you turn right along the lane. After 300 yds the lane turns sharp right by Hunters Lodge. Take the path to the left marked 'Belbroughton Road ½'. Keep the hedge on the left as you go down the hill.

At the bottom of the slope go through the trees, through a wicket gate and across the wet valley bottom to emerge into a large open field. Climb up the field edge to the road at another gate adjacent to a bungalow.

It will now probably be two hours or more since the start of your walk and you may wish to make a diversion into Blakedown to the left for a pub stop — The Old House at Home is about ten minutes away. Otherwise go straight across the road and down an obvious path with woods to the right and a house to the left. Keep the woods to your right maintaining the same direction as you emerge into an open field. At the end of the field is a house and gate (Broome Mill). Go to the left of the gate and follow the path which wanders to the left of the drive to the house, eventually coming out onto the drive which is followed up to the main road.

Taking due care, cross the road, turn right for a few yards and then left at the side of a farmhouse, Harborough Farm. Keep straight on along the surfaced track until it bends sharply to the left. Here carry straight on following the hedge-line on the right. The path drops into Stakenbridge to emerge onto a road: turn left along this road, NOT up the marked path on the immediate left. Instead go under the railway bridge, cross the road very carefully and turn right just beyond the pool onto a clear well laid track.

Cross a stile and go up to the right of the conifers, following a stream and coming out onto a metalled surface just in front of a house. Keep straight on, coming out at Brakemill Farm.

If you go a little way right along the road here you will reach an old mill, now converted into a residence. The old water-wheel has been restored.

Returning to our main route, keep straight on over the road with the house to the left and barns to the right. Continue up the track with a hedge on the right.

The path now goes through a gate into a narrow lane between two hedgerows, then emerges onto another metalled road. Turn right here, then left up the marked footpath which is part of the North Worcestershire Path. Go up the field with a fence on the left and a large house, 'The Birches', up to the right and surrounded with trees.

The path goes up to the left of these trees and turns right behind them at stiles at the corner. From here there is a good view of the obelisk on Wychbury Hill (if it has not fallen down! It is in a very precarious state.) The path now descends towards Hagley with an excellent view of the Clent Hills. Throughout this section we follow the North Worcestershire Path way-marks — small yellow triangles on the footpath markers.

We soon cross to the other side of the hedge, cross the railway and emerge into a housing estate on Hagley's outskirts.

After crossing the railway bridge, turn right and immediately left, following the road up to its end. Here we join a footpath, again alongside a stream. Go straight across the main B4187 and follow the footpath sign 'Hagley ½' crossing seven stiles to come into Hagley itself. Cross the main road by the car showroom to join the Bromsgrove Road.

➡ GR 914808. *Join the walk here if you are starting from Hagley.*

Go down the road, due south, about 200 yds to the first road (Hall Lane) on the left (opposite the Lyttleton Arms). Turn down this and after a further 250 yds, at the road junction and just before the entrance to Hagley Hall, take the marked footpath to the right. Look out here for the old drinking fountain, dated 1914, and inscribed 'Keep the pavement dry'! We are still following the North Worcestershire Path, observing the way-marks on this very well used path. Running parallel for a while is an equally well used bridleway.

With a fine view of the Hall on the left we soon come to a footpath division as the way crosses a ditch. Keep to the main path between the fences, ignoring the stile on the right and the private road to the left.

After another quarter mile there is another footpath division where the North Worcestershire Path turns left. Our way lies ahead, going half right down a narrow path between iron railings, past a pond, across a private drive to Home Farm, and emerging onto a road, where we bear left.

Keep straight on past the Fountain pub and along Odnall Lane to the crossroads by Clent church. Approaching the crossroads and just past School House on the right you can join the short waterside

'Elsie Partington Walk'. If you look back at this point you will see a fine dovecote in the grounds of Clent Cottage.

We go straight on at the crossroads, but the walk could clearly be extended by making a diversion along the footpaths across the Clent Hills or Walton Hill.

Our road, signposted Walton Pool, is followed for ½ mile to the T-junction, where we turn left and then right down a track leading to Walton Farm and signposted Calcot Hill. Passing in front of the farm we soon top the rise and turn right down a track marked 'Private Road to Moor Hall Farm, Footpath only to main road'. When the track turns left, near to two pools, keep straight on through a gate with a hedge on your right, maintaining a south-westerly direction to the stile on the main road. This is where we started, eleven miles ago (unless you used the alternative starting point from Hagley, in which case now continue from the first paragraph).

8

Earlswood Lakes
by
Peter Groves

A stroll through the Clowes Wood Nature Reserve and around the three tree lined pools which make up the reservoir feeding the Stratford Canal.

MAPS: Landranger 139
Pathfinder 954 (SP07/17)
CAR PARKING: Earlswood
RAILWAY STATION: Earlswood (Birmingham, Snow Hill to Stratford line)
START & FINISH: Earlswood station (GR 097743)
DISTANCE: 4½ miles

This is a circular walk starting from Earlswood railway station where there is parking for British Rail passengers and also roadside parking.

From Earlswood station turn right and walk about a hundred yards down Rumbush Lane to reach a stile and signposted footpath on the right. Turn right along this path, passing between a hedge and a fence, to reach Clowes Wood which you enter by a stile.

Clowes Wood is a nature reserve covering seventy-three acres and owned by the Warwickshire Nature Conservation Trust. It supports a varied flora and fauna in woodland, heathland, a meadow, ditches, streams and ponds. Over fifty species of fungi have been recorded and fifty-four species of birds, including wood warbler, woodcock, sparrow-hawk and all three British woodpeckers. The woodland includes oak, birch, beech, alder and rowan. Flowers to look out for include wild lily-of-the-valley, bluebells, wood anemone, wood sage, wild angelica and foxglove.

Clowes Wood, together with the Earlswood Lakes, is designated as a Site of Special Scientific Interest (SSSI).

The wood is criss-crossed by a multitude of paths. We shall keep to the perimeter but there are lots of opportunities for exploring deeper into the wood.

In the wood, immediately turn right along a well defined path and walk round the edge of the wood. This will bring you to a footbridge over a stream which you cross and continue forward: over to your right you will see a footbridge crossing the railway line. This will take you into another part of the wood if you want to explore further. Our walk will, however, continue along the path, which now swings left, accompanied by the railway line on the right.

Eventually the path swings round left away from the railway which is now passing along a high embankment. You soon meet a narrow meadow on the right — this is an old hay-meadow which has been mown and grazed for over 200 years. About 40 yds. past the end of this take the path which branches off to the right. It is reinforced underfoot with logs to make it more passable when the ground is muddy.

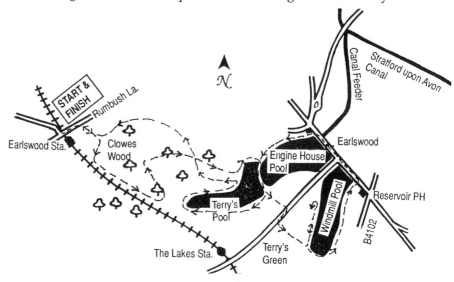

The path will bring you to two footbridges, which you cross. Turn right and walk along the main path with a stream to your right, ignoring any minor paths. This will bring you to another footbridge: cross this and turn left along the first of the three Earlswood lakes, Terry's Pool. Earlswood Lakes are wholly artificial and were created to provide a water supply to the nearby Stratford Canal. This canal, authorised by an Act of Parliament of 1793, runs from its junction with the Worcester and Birmingham Canal at Kings Norton to Stratford-on-Avon where it joins the River Avon.

Continue walking around Terry's Pool until you reach a bridge on your right. This will take you onto the dam which separates Terry's Pool from Engine House Pool. Cross the dam noting, as you approach the end, a paddle which enables water to be transferred into Engine House Pool from Terry's Pool. Cross a bridge and through a kissing gate into a recreation area and a car park. Go through the car park and between houses onto the road. Turn right here.

About 150 yards along the road you will find on the left a track marked with a footpath sign (though this sign is rather obscured by the hedge). Walk along this track to reach a kissing gate on the left which leads to our third lake, Windmill Pool.

Engine House Pool

To your left is a footbridge leading to a path along the western side of the pool. Unfortunately this is a cul-de-sac for it leads only to a sailing club. However, the path along the lake-side is a very pleasant one with some nice views across the water, so it is worth walking even though you will have to turn back when you reach the gate into the sailing club.

Back at the footbridge turn left and continue along the pool. Cross another footbridge which goes over an overflow channel and turn left along the east side of the pool. A brook now accompanies you to your right.

The path will bring you through a gate onto the road: turn left to walk along the main dam (the Reservoir public house is to the right if you are in need of refreshment). Half-way along the dam a causeway brings in a road from the left. If you look around here you will see the overflows which take excess water into the brook along which we were walking earlier. This brook feeds into the River Blythe about a mile away at Cheswick Green.

Past the causeway we are again walking beside Engine House Pool. Carry on to the north corner of this where you will see the engine house which pumps water to the Stratford Canal about half a mile distant. You can see the feeder channel if you cross the road. There was originally a beam engine here (which explains the height of the building) but that has now been replaced by electric pumps.

A kissing gate will take you to a path along the lake-side which leads to the bridge and dam that you crossed earlier. Cross this again and then turn right through an iron gate to walk around Terry's Pool. Ignoring any paths off to the left continue around the lake until your path takes you over a footbridge. Immediately after crossing this turn left over another footbridge into Clowes Wood.

Go forward along the main track, ignoring a branch to the right, with a small stream accompanying you on the left. As we saw earlier there are numerous small paths which criss-cross the wood. Ignore these and keep going in a generally westerly direction. The path through the wood has at some time been waymarked with white paint on the trees, though some of the marks have now faded somewhat.

When you meet the footbridge (leading to another footbridge) that you crossed earlier don't cross this again but carry on straight ahead. The path meanders around and will soon bring you to a branch to the left leading in a few yards to a footbridge and a Nature Reserve sign. Cross the bridge and turn right along a well defined path which will bring you to the right hand edge of the wood. Avoid any temptation to go into the wood, continuing on around the edge.

Eventually you will meet a stile on the right leading into a field. This is the one that you crossed at the start of the walk. Go over it again and up through the fields to reach Rumbush Lane. Turn left to return to Earlswood station.

9

Lapworth to Warwick
by
John Bach

A ramble through the Warwickshire countryside along the Grand Union Canal,
passing the spectacular Hatton flight of twenty-one locks.

MAPS: Landranger 139 and 151
Pathfinder 954(SP07/17), 975(SP06/16), 976(SP26/36)
CAR PARKS: Broome Hall Lane (Picnic site/Car park); Lapworth, Hatton and Warwick
Railway Stations
RAILWAY STATIONS: Lapworth, Hatton, Warwick
START: Lapworth (GR 187709)
FINISH: Warwick (GR 276662)
DISTANCE: 9 miles approx. Add approx. 3 miles if return is to Hatton.

We start on the Stratford Canal at lock no. 19 which you will find by the Broome Hall picnic site where there is parking. *If you are coming from Lapworth station turn right outside the station and go down to the B4439, turn right and take the first left over the canal bridge (Broome Hall Lane). A "P" sign will direct you into the picnic site.* Go straight through the car park onto the canal towpath opposite two canal reservoirs. Turn right towards the canal junction and cross over bridge no. 36. Note the split in the middle of the bridge which was to allow the tow-rope to pass through for horse-drawn boats.

Turn right, passing through a gate, to join the southern section of the Stratford Canal alongside lock no. 21. As you walk down the path you will see a barrel-roofed cottage, originally occupied by the lock keeper. This style of cottage is typical of this section of the canal. The gate leading into a yard beside the cottage is of an interesting design.

Continue along the towpath to lock no. 25 and then turn left down a drive. Before you leave the canal note the diamond shaped sign on your left which details permitted bridge weights for vehicles. To your right you will see another barrel-roofed cottage, Kingswood Cottage.

After passing Kingswood Cottage and crossing a stream you will find yourself in Dick's Lane. Continue along the full length of this, passing under a railway bridge, until you reach a T-junction. At the junction

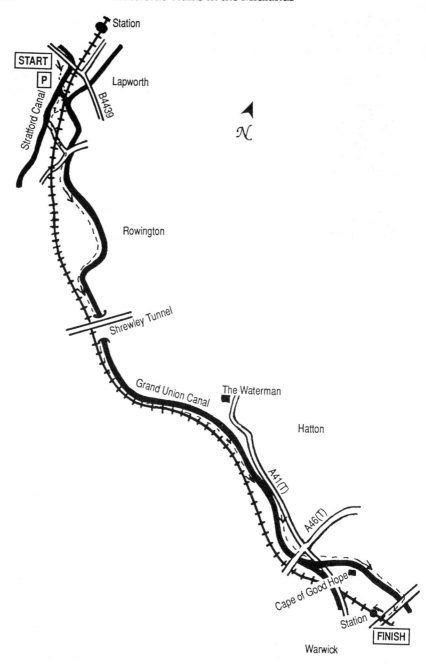

turn left and walk up the hill — but do not cross the bridge (except perhaps to visit the 'Tom-o'-Wood'). Pass through the gate on your right to join the towpath and turn right along this.

A 'split bridge' on the Stratford Canal

You are now on the Grand Union Canal which links Birmingham and London. Here the path is quite wide as the canal contours round a hillside before entering a cutting which, in wet weather, can be very muddy. As you pass under bridge no. 62, up above two long distance paths cross the canal — the Heart of England Way and the West Midland Way. From here the canal crosses a valley on a high embankment with good views on either side. The view to your right is worth studying for when you pass under bridge no. 61 (White Bridge) you can look back towards bridge no. 62 which you passed some time ago. This will give you some idea of just how much the canal twists and turns and why the path should, if possible, be walked both ways to appreciate all the contours and views. This section of the canal was completely rebuilt during the winter of 1987-88. It is now attractively landscaped and the towpath has been planted with trees and bushes. Here you are walking through pure traditional Warwickshire countryside — no prairie farming to be seen!

Just past bridge 60 you cross a weir which takes excess water from the canal along a channel to a little stream below. Just beyond is a sluice enabling this section of canal to be drained if necessary for repairs. A little further on you pass an old abandoned weir.

Set into the concrete on the edge of the canal you will see the date 1933. The Grand Union Canal, with the aid of a Government grant, was widened and modernised in the 1930s. Unfortunately the task was never completed and this attempt to prevent the commercial decline of the canal failed.

A typical 'roses and castles' design on a canal narrow boat

The next point of interest is Shrewley Tunnel — 433 yards long. There is no towpath passing through this and the path goes over the hill. As you leave the canal in a cutting the towpath goes through its own tunnel. This is the way the horses came, leaving the boatmen to 'leg' their boats through the tunnel. On leaving the tunnel you have a steady climb to the road. If you wish to visit the 'Durham Ox' turn right and continue on a few yards, crossing a high railway bridge. The Ox is then on your left.

The walk continues straight ahead along a path on the opposite side of the road and soon rejoins the canal. As you pass under bridge no. 56, Hatton Station is to your right — this rail link is useful if you want to cut your walk short or extend it, as I will describe later.

The next mile is uneventful except for a pretty garden at bridge no.55. At this bridge you will see a sign indicating that you are now on the Hatton Farm Trail which you might like to walk on another occasion. From here you continue to the top of the Hatton 21 flight of locks. Do not rush this section for the surrounding countryside is particularly attractive.

The towpath changes sides at bridge no. 54 beside the Hatton Maintenance Yard. Refreshments are available here at 'The Waterman', which you can reach by going over the stile at the left of the British Waterways office and up through the field into the pub garden.

Before you leave bridge no. 54 study the position of the distant St Mary's Church, Warwick in relation to the line of the locks. The church was probably used to align the locks when they were first being constructed in the 1790s.

You are now about to descend the famous (or notorious!) Hatton flight of twenty-one locks. In a distance of two miles they take the canal down 150 ft. They were all widened as part of the 1930s improvements and the remains of the old locks can be see beside the new ones where they form the overflow weirs. Each lock holds about 50,000 gallons of water.

As you walk down the flight of locks you may wish to give a boat crew a hand for they have their work cut out between bridges nos. 54 and 53! Thereafter the locks are more spaced out.

Just past lock 29 you should be able to see the tower of Budbrooke Church to your right. Years ago Budbrooke was the home barracks of the Warwickshire Regiment but there is little evidence of this these days.

Lock 26 is Hatton Bottom lock. There is a picnic area here and car parking. You are now on the outskirts of Warwick with houses and factories nearby.

Just before bridge no. 51, Budbrooke Junction, the main canal goes left. Opposite is the Saltisford Arm leading to moorings and boat facilities, and also to a Visitor Centre and a wild flower garden. There is no towpath along the arm but if you want to visit the centre and the garden you can reach them by road.

At the next lock you will find 'The Cape of Good Hope'. You will have to walk over the lock gates to reach the pub — somewhat tricky if you have small children or a dog with you. From the pub it is just over a mile to Warwick. Another possibility, which I recommend, is to do an about-turn here, walk back up the Hatton flight and then to Hatton Station for your return. This will add another enjoyable three miles to your walk.

But for Warwick continue along the canal to bridge 49, go up to the road, cross the canal and go straight forward to reach the town centre. Warwick Castle is worth a visit if you have time.

For the railway station take the road on the right immediately before the railway bridge, then about fifty yards along here take the steps to the left which lead up to the station.

10

Wombourne
by
Peter Groves

This walk through the Staffordshire countryside includes a section of the Stafford-shire and Worcestershire canal, the unique Bratch locks, and part of the disused Kingswinford Railway, now converted into an attractive walkway.

MAPS: Landranger 139
Pathfinder 912(SO89/99)
CAR PARKING: Bratch Locks picnic site.
BUSES: West Midlands 556, Wolverhampton - Stourbridge. *From the bus stop in Bull Meadow Lane walk along Billy Bunns Lane, passing under the old railway bridge, to reach Bratch Locks.*
START & FINISH: Bratch Locks (GR 867938)
DISTANCE: 9½ miles

Before starting our walk it is worth spending a few minutes reading the canal information board which you will find in the picnic area adjacent to the car park.

Then, from the car park go across the canal bridge and turn right onto the canal towpath. This is the Staffordshire and Worcestershire Canal, built by James Brindley to link Midlands towns to the River Severn, which it joins at Stourport. Although the canal mostly follows the gentle contours of the land there is, at Bratch, a considerable change of level which required Brindley to construct a unique set of three very closely spaced locks, opened in 1772. These you will see ahead of you with, to the right, the octagonal building which is generally considered to be a toll house. Certainly it conforms to the general pattern of toll houses built by Brindley along this canal, although, as you may have read on the canal information board in the picnic area, there is some doubt about its actual purpose.

The distance between the top and bottom gates of adjacent locks is only four feet. On the opposite side of the road to the first lock you will see one of the two side ponds which provide a supply of water to the two lower locks. Water runs into these as the higher lock is emptied, and runs out to fill the lower lock. The closeness of the gates, and the problems of manipulating the water supply can present problems of

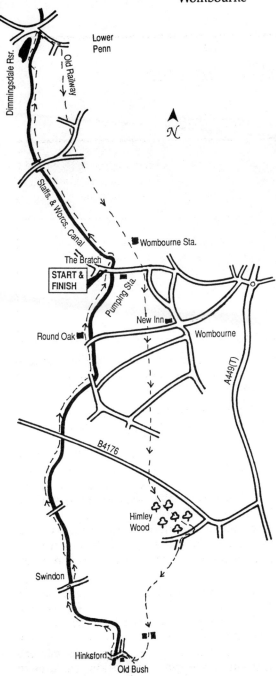

navigation for less experienced boaters. Although today most locks are unmanned the presence of a lock-keeper is very necessary at Bratch!

You may notice some foam on the surface of the water in the locks. The outflow from Wolverhampton Sewage Works runs into the canal and although this has been purified some amount of detergent seems to remain. This source of water has proved invaluable in times of severe drought, enabling this stretch of the Staffs. and Worcester. to remain open when other canals have had to be closed.

Walk past the locks, the towpath crossing to the right side of the canal. Our walk for the next 1¾ miles will take us north through some pleasant Staffordshire countryside, the canal winding around as Brindley kept as long as he could to a contour, so increasing the length of the canal but avoiding the need for locks, tunnels or embankments except when the topography of the

Bratch locks

ground made these inevitable. The only scar on the landscape is the rows of electricity pylons that can be seen ahead. We shall have a more dramatic view of these later.

Awbridge Lock, which we soon meet, is crossed by a beautiful brick bridge. This was built by Brindley and is, sadly, the only original canal bridge that we shall meet on our walk. To the right of the lock is an attractive circular weir which carries excess water around the lock. The Staffs. and Worcester Canal is characterised by an interesting series of weirs, varying considerably in design from lock to lock. Look out for these as you continue your walk.

At Dimmingsdale Lock the towpath changes sides and to the left you now pass a canal reservoir, a haunt of water birds.

Leave the canal at Dimmingsdale bridge (No. 53). Go up to the road and turn right to cross the bridge. Take the right fork in the road, signposted Lower Penn. Then ignore the right hand turn to Wombourne and continue straight ahead to reach a bridge over the old Kingswinford Railway. Just before the bridge take the footpath to the left and when you reach a fence turn right to go under the bridge.

The railway was built by the Great Western Railway between 1912 and 1925 to connect Wolverhampton with Kingswinford. Like the canal it followed the valley of the Smestow Brook (which we shall see later). It has now been converted into a walkway and bridle path, with numerous picnic spots, and we shall follow it south for about three miles. It is attractively wooded and well tenanted with birds, wild flowers and flowering shrubs. It is particularly lovely in the Spring.

The cutting soon gives way to an embankment, and a bridge takes you across the road. From here you will get the dramatic view of a forest of electricity pylons. See how many of them you can count!

Some two miles along the walkway you meet the well preserved Wombourne Station. Just beyond is bridge No. 33 and if you wish to end your walk here it is a short distance to the car park at Bratch. To leave the walkway you need to continue on over the bridge and after about 100 yds, just before reaching some houses, take the path to the left (which is easy to miss). This will bring you down onto Station Road. Turn left along here, then left again under the bridge to return to the car park.

Awbridge Bridge — the oldest bridge on the canal

Continuing along the walkway you soon pass through a particularly beautiful cutting in which the trees on either side of the track have grown across to form a green archway.

On reaching bridge 31 you have an opportunity for a pub break in Wombourne. To reach the pub, carry on for about 50 yds and take the path on the right which climbs up to the road. Cross the bridge and a few hundred yards along on the left, at the road junction, you will find the New Inn which serves bar food Monday to Friday.

Continuing southwards, the path crosses a surfaced track past bridge 29 and then goes through a little tunnel. We now leave Wombourne behind us to go through another tree-lined cutting in the red Bunter Sandstone. After passing under the B4176 at bridge 26, and as the path leaves the cutting for level ground, we pass through Himley Wood.

Just past a picnic table on the right we meet a sign announcing that we are at the site of Himley station, though all traces of the station buildings have now disappeared. Take the surfaced track on the right which leads down to the road. Turn right along this road and then, after about 100 yds, where the road swings right, go straight ahead along the farm road through the field.

When you reach a row of trees the track swings left. Cross a stile here to continue along the track to the farm, soon passing ponds on the left and right. Past the second pond go through a gate into the farmyard. Where the main track swings right go ahead, passing between two black corrugated iron barns and a wooden barn on the left and the old farmhouse on the right. Go through a gate into a field and cross this diagonally, aiming for another gate ahead. Passing through the gate cross a stream and turn right to walk alongside it.

Go over a stile and across the next field, still keeping the stream on your right. As you approach a building, swing left to reach a stile in the corner of the field beside a white house. Cross the road (beside the Old Bush Inn) and go along the road opposite, signed Hinksford Park (a caravan park). Pass on the right the South Staffordshire Hinksford Pumping Station, built in 1900 and with its brickwork still in immaculate condition.

Cross the canal bridge (No. 38), turn right onto the towpath and go left along this, passing the pumping station. We are now back on the Staffs. and Worcester Canal.

Hinksford Lock, which you soon meet, has an interestingly shaped weir — you will have to cross to the other side of the lock to see it.

At Swindon Lock the towpath changes sides for a short distance. This is because there was originally an ironworks on the left side which pre-dated the building of the canal. Previously there had been a corn mill here, powered by the Smestow Brook which runs close to the canal. The mill was converted into an iron works in 1647 but this closed in 1976 and has now been replaced by a housing estate. However, if you study the opposite bank of the canal you can see that it is brick reinforced — an indication of the position of the old ironworks wharf.

The bridge at Marsh Lock is a 'split bridge', the gap in the centre of the bridge being designed to allow the towing ropes of horse-drawn boats to pass through. The towpath here regains the left side of the canal. Below, on the left, is the Smestow Brook.

At Botterham bridge (No.42) we meet two 'staircase' locks, so named because the top gate of the lower lock is also the bottom gate of the upper lock.

At Houndel Bridge (No. 45) the towpath passes the Round Oak pub where you have further opportunities for food (lunchtime and evening meals) and refreshment. Bumble Hole Lock, a little further on, is interesting for its fine brick bridge, unspoilt lock cottage and another oddly shaped weir.

It is now only a short distance to Bratch where you cross the bridge to the car park or to walk to Bull Meadow Lane to catch the bus. But before you leave spend a little time studying the Bratch Pumping Station (just past the car park) with its delightfully eccentric design, dating from 1895.

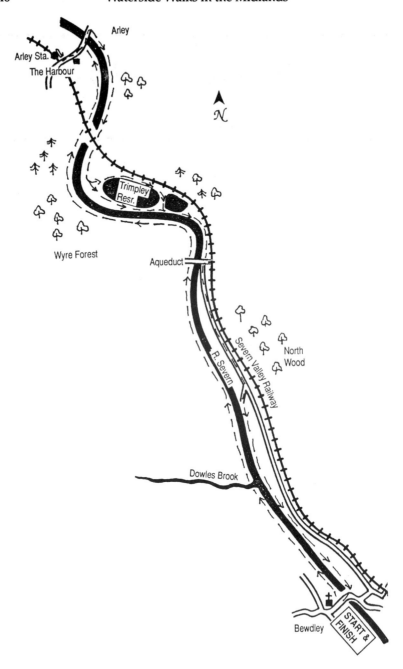

11
Bewdley and Arley
by
Mark Linley

The Severn is the Midlands' most distinguished river and this walk takes you along one bank from Bewdley to Arley, then returns along the opposite bank. Alternatively you can return to Bewdley by steam train on the Severn Valley Railway (but check first that there is a service running on the day that you intend to do your walk).

MAPS: Landranger: 138
Pathfinder: 952 (SO67/77). 932 (SO68/78)
CAR PARK: Load Street, Bewdley.
BUSES: Midland Red West; X92 Birmingham — Hereford.
RAILWAY: Severn Railway. Bridgnorth — Kidderminster. Phone Bewdley (0299) 401001 for times.
START & FINISH: Bewdley (GR 785754)
DISTANCE: 7½ miles. 3¾ miles if you return from Arley by train.

This walk starts at Load Street car park in Bewdley. The car park is opposite the fire station and can be reached from the main road or from Bridgnorth Road.

Bewdley is a small town which was of great importance from Saxon times when it was the gateway to Wales through the nearby Wyre Forest. It was a thriving inland port until the Staffordshire and Worcestershire canal, completed in 1772, took much of the commercial traffic away to nearby Stourport. The surrounding land was owned by a few very wealthy and influential families, among them Richard, Duke of York (b. 1425). Royalty frequently visited and stayed in the area. Bewdley has remained remarkably free of modern developments and still retains a number of old timber framed buildings together with many elegant eighteenth and nineteenth century structures. It is worth spending a little time exploring the town when you have completed your walk.

The town's prosperity continued until Queen Victoria's reign when, as well as the continuing drop in river traffic, trades like skin tanning and charcoal burning died out, and boat building declined. Today it is known as a beauty spot: fortunately the former traffic jams, so common in the holiday seasons, have been relieved by the opening in 1987 of the Bewdley by-pass.

The walk starts along the bank of the River Severn at a point opposite Bewdley Rowing Club across the river. As you will see from markers on the stiles we are here on part of the Worcestershire Way, a long distance footpath which runs from Kinver to Malvern. The track is easy to follow and is man-made for the first stretch.

After climbing a stile Dowles Manor can be seen to the left ahead. This is an impressive building dating from 1607. It stands on a hill on the edge of the Wyre Forest.

Bewdley

Ahead are the remains of the old Wyre Forest Railway viaduct, long abandoned. Just before reaching this we cross the Dowles Brook which sweeps down from the forest to join the Severn. This brook gurgles its way for five miles through the forest and has a high oxygen content which makes it one of the few streams in the Midlands where freshwater crayfish can be found. In recent years, however, these have declined due to some pollution and the use of pesticides. A few years ago these creatures were easy to find, but not so now. Also, at that time, kingfishers were to be seen on most days. These too have declined, in this case due to the loss of their main food, small brown trout. The trout have been devastated by wild mink which reached this area in the middle 1980s and caused havoc. These animals, descended from escaped ranch specimens bred for their fur, are deadly predators of animal, bird and fish.

Along the next mile or so, where the forest reaches down to the river, it is possible to hear the mocking laugh-like call of the green woodpecker. This bird can be recognised by its undulating flight. Close up it is full of bright colours — red topped head, yellow rump, green and brown-barred wing and tail feathers. At a distance it seems tawny brown that blends with the tree background. If you keep quiet you may see one coming down on wood ants which it picks up from their nests with its long sticky tongue.

Green woodpecker

This part of the forest is also the home of the great spotted woodpecker which is red, white and black. You can hear the machine gun-like sounds it makes as it hammers holes in trees.

Another occupant of the forest is the rare lesser spotted woodpecker. This bird is the size of a sparrow and has reddish spots and stripes against a dark background. Along the river bank you might see heron and wagtails. Swans, which used to be very common, have almost disappeared — perhaps due to poisoning by fishermen's lead weights.

About a mile past the old viaduct the river is crossed by an aqueduct carrying water from the Elan Valley to Birmingham. A little further on, the river bends to the left through Seckley Woods which is part of the Wyre Forest. On the opposite river bank can be seen a high ridge which conceals two reservoirs — we shall see these on the way back.

After rounding a bend you will see the Victoria Bridge, built in 1861 for the Great Western Railway and now carrying the Severn Valley Railway which operates standard gauge steam trains between Bridgenorth and Kidderminster.

At Arley the Severn is crossed by a footbridge. This replaced an old chain ferry, remains of which can still be seen. After reaching the bridge turn left on the road that will take you to the Harbour public house, immediately on your left, or to Arley Railway Station.

Arley Station is on the Severn Valley line and is kept in superb condition by voluntary workers. The staff at this beautiful station are most helpful and take great pride in their work. The waiting room houses some of the awards they have won for the best station in the country. You can obtain refreshments here at reasonable prices, and can sit in the superb gardens which have tables and chairs and give a wonderful view down over the Severn and across to Arley.

In a meadow across the river can be seen a small herd of Highland cattle which are worth closer study. These animals are descended from ancient herds and are very interesting. They are long haired with a fringe dangling over forehead and upper face. Look out for the one huge bull with the group.

At this point you can return to Bewdley by train if you wish to forego the remainder of the walk.

The walk back begins from Arley after crossing the footbridge over the Severn and turning right. The track can be clearly seen and is followed through Eymore Wood alongside the river. Follow the path until it comes out on open ground before the reservoir embankment. It is worth leaving the footpath to climb up, then walk around the reservoirs. The large one is used for yachting. Both are flanked by woods and there is a good view all round. Rejoin the footpath and continue along the river bank.

The path rises and you soon meet again the Elan Valley pipeline. Looking to the left you will see the cutting through the trees that marks the line of this on its way to Birmingham. Unfortunately the footpath comes to an end here due to the intrusion of privately owned land. Continue forward along the road for about a mile until, shortly past a telephone box, a track goes off to the right. Turn along this but almost immediately cross a stile on the left into a field. Go down the right side of this and a stile will bring you back to the river again.

A few hundred yards past the old railway viaduct look out for the markers indicating water level. The Severn is notorious for flooding and the markers give an indication of how high this can sometimes be.

We enter Bewdley through an attractively laid out public garden, the path going behind the buildings of the Bewdley Rowing Club and out onto the superb stone three arched bridge, built by Thomas Telford in 1788 to replace an earlier medieval bridge. Walk across the bridge to the town.

Across the bridge you can either turn right along a lane to Load Street or walk on down the main road and take a short cut between the George Hotel and the medical centre. Both will bring you to the car park.

12

An Avon Saunter from 'Drunken Bidford'
by
John Newson

The Warwickshire village of Bidford-on-Avon in Shakespeare country is reputed to have been the famous Bard's favourite drinking haunt — hence the name 'Drunken Bidford'. This circular ramble takes in a pleasant stretch of the River Avon together with some good views from Cleeve Hill and the charming village of Cleeve Prior.

> MAPS: Landranger 150
> Pathfinder: 997 (SP05/15), 1020 (SP04/14)
> CAR PARK: Riverside, Bidford (Adjacent to Bidford Bridge).
> BUS: Birmingham - Bidford. Midland Red 146 and X6.
> START and FINISH: Bidford on Avon (GR 099517)
> DISTANCE: 9½ miles

Go through the car park beside Bidford Bridge and along a track leading to changing rooms for the adjacent sports grounds. Past the changing rooms this becomes a footpath which skirts round the left side of the grounds, the River Avon being away over to your right. Continue along this path, then go through a kissing gate and across a field. Cross a stile and walk along the left-hand edge of a second field. Cross a stile in the hedge to the left, over a ditch, and then continue along the right-hand edge of two further fields. Another stile will take you alongside some houses to the lane at Temple Farm, Marlcliff.

Continue along the lane for a few yards and then turn first right to follow a signposted bridleway. This will take you to the River Avon. Continue on the same bridleway (which soon becomes concreted) until you reach a weir and a lock. The lock is new, having being re-built when the Avon was made navigable again a few years ago. At the weir go over a stile and continue along the riverside for about three miles.

After about a quarter of a mile you will see the little River Arrow joining the Avon on the right. Beyond is the tower of Salford Priors church.

When you reach a wood look out for a stile on the right which takes the footpath down closer to the river's edge. The path, now running along the foot of Cleeve Hill, is particularly attractive though subject to erosion in places. It is liable to become rather muddy if the weather

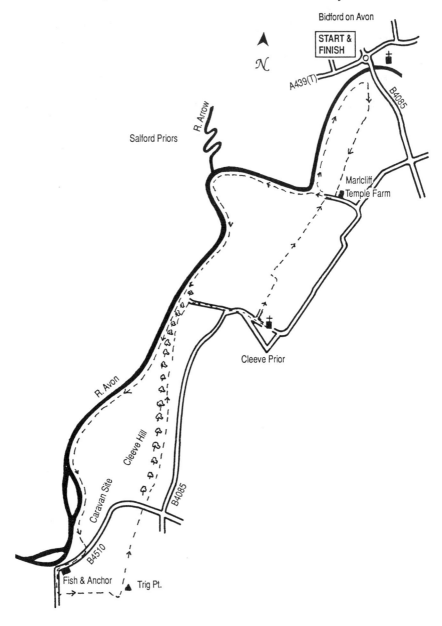

The bridge over the Avon at Bidford

has been bad. Eventually you will reach a second weir: this is a very picturesque spot.

Very soon after passing the weir you will see a lock cutting on the right and, a little way along it, one of the original locks. This was subject to silting up and with the restoration of the Avon navigation it was abandoned and a new lock built. The new lock (beside an old mill) and the new lock cutting are on the right, about a quarter of a mile beyond the weir as you approach a caravan site.

Go through the caravan site to reach a road (B4510). Turn right along this and in a few yards you will reach the Fish and Anchor Inn (meals but no bar snacks). You have now walked four miles.

From the pub, walk about 150 yds along the B4510, then turn left taking a signed wide path. This crosses another path, then swings right and ascends Cleeve Hill. At the top turn left along a track, then immediately sharp left again along a path beside a gate. Ignore the remains of a stile to the left and go straight forward, soon passing a water tower on your right. There is a trig point close to this, but difficult to see.

The path now follows the ridge in a north-easterly direction with some good views of the Avon. After about half a mile it crosses a road (B4510), passes to the right of a bungalow, and continues in the same direction for just over a mile, passing through Cleeve Prior Nature Reserve. This is a delightful wood-side walk. Reaching a lane you will see a board describing the Nature Reserve which was opened in 1983 by Lord Melchett, past president of the Ramblers Association.

Turn right down the lane into Cleeve Prior village to visit the village church of St Andrew. The doorways of this church are Norman, the nave thirteenth century, the chancel probably fourteenth century, and the font also probably fourteenth century with a much older base. There are two fragments of fifteenth century glass in the north-east window of the nave. In the garden of a house close to the church there is a fine piece of topiary.

Cleeve Prior

After visiting the church retrace your steps and turn right into Froglands Lane. Follow this lane, which becomes a bridleway, to a junction of ways. Turn left along the path signed 'Public footpath to river ½' and go straight ahead, crossing another path, to emerge onto the Cleeve Hill ridge with more fine views towards the River Avon. Turn right and continue along this ridge path for just over a mile before dropping down steeply into Marlcliff.

At Marlcliff turn left through a wicket gate to the left of a thatched cottage. Go forward a few yards and turn left along the bridleway (that you walked along earlier) to reach the river. Turn right here and follow the riverside path back to Bidford-on-Avon.

13

The River Severn and the Droitwich Canal

by
Clive Hough

This walk is suitable either as a gentle summer afternoon stroll or as a brisk short day's walk in winter. It features a lovely stretch of Britain's greatest river, the Severn, and the canal, opened in 1777, which links Droitwich to the Severn. The scenery is charming.

MAPS: Landranger 150
Pathfinder 974 (SO86/96)
BUSES: Midland Red West X93 Birmingham to Kidderminster and Worcester via Holt Heath,
Return — Midland Red West 144 Droitwich to Birmingham, Bromsgrove and Worcester:
X43 Droitwich to Birmingham and Worcester
START: Holt Heath (GR 815632)
FINISH: Droitwich (GR 903635)
DISTANCE: 9 miles

From the Red Lion pub at Holt Heath walk about half a mile east along the A4133 until you reach the bridge over the River Severn at Holt Fleet. Take care as this is a busy road.

Holt Fleet is a favourite boating and fishing resort, quite lively on summer week-ends.

Cross the bridge to the north bank of the river and descend to the towpath. Walk east, the river on your right, past the Wharf Inn. For the next mile and a half we follow the river, going across the odd stile now and then. This section is quite picturesque. The Norman church and the ancient castle of Holt can soon be seen on the opposite bank. Although much of the castle is now modern the tower is fourteenth century.

Keep on the riverside path until you reach an old ferry crossing point where the path crosses a stile and turns away from the river. A short enclosed path of about 30 yds, with an old boat-house on the right, leads to a driveway. Turn left on this drive and follow it as it bends to the right, uphill, to reach the A449(T). Cross this road with care to the verge

opposite. Turn right
and walk for about 100
yds until you see a pub-
lic footpath sign
marked Chatley on the
left.

Cross a stile and im-
mediately drop down
to the left to another
stile into a field. Turn
right and walk with the
hedge on your right to
the field corner.

Cross the stile and,
keeping on the same
line, walk straight
ahead across the arable
field to another stile
beside a gate. Cross
this and continue for-
ward with the hedge
on your right. As you
top the small rise Caves
Farm is visible ahead.
Just before reaching a
barn here cross the stile
by a gate on your right
and walk to the gate at
the corner of the field.
Go through this to
reach a lane and the
hamlet of Chatley.

Turn left on this lane
and then turn right
onto a bridleway sign-
posted 'Egg Lane'.
After 10 yds turn left
off the farm drive along
a track with a hedge on
the left. The way de-
scends slightly and
bends left. Cross a
stream at the bottom of
the incline and turn

Old mill on the River Salwarpe

right along the edge of a field.

Where the path forks go right and keep along the right-hand hedge to go through a gate. Keep on the same line to cross a footbridge.

Turn left and walk with a fence on your right, passing a former mill. Turn left over another footbridge over a weir. You are now in the valley of the little River Salwarpe and the path through here is particularly pleasant.

After crossing the bridge follow the river, which is on your right, until a small stream comes in from the left. Follow this stream to its source in a pond and continue forward, with Tapenhall Farm on the left, to emerge onto a lane through a gate at the field corner.

Turn right and walk down the winding lane to Porter's Mill, now converted into dwellings. Continue towards a canal bridge and turn left just before reaching it to go north along another lane. The reeded Droitwich Canal is now on your right. Join its towpath by a gate on the right as the lane bears left.

The Droitwich Canal was principally used in the late eighteenth and the nineteenth centuries for carrying salt from the pits around Droitwich. The little River Salwarpe was too winding and shallow to be made navigable so the canal was built to link the town to the Severn. Opened in 1777 it differs from most other Midland canals in that the locks were built 14 ft wide to take the barges specially designed to use this canal and the River Severn. Although largely derelict for most of this century it is now being restored.

As you follow the towpath you pass two locks which, at the time of writing, are being restored by the Droitwich Canal Trust. As you get nearer to Droitwich, and in the town itself, you will see further signs of the extensive work that has been done by the Trust. The third and fourth locks that you pass are now restored, complete with new balance beams.

Eventually the canal bends sharp right in a cutting and the tower of Salwarpe church is visible ahead. As you near the village look out for steps leading down to a stile at the bottom of the embankment to your left. Go over this and turn right to cross another stile by a gate leading onto the road in Salwarpe village. This is a charming and quiet place, being made even more so by not being on a through road.

Turn right and then enter the churchyard on the left. The church is partly Norman, prettily set on a wooded rise. Take time to seek out the old flight of steps leading down to the River Salwarpe at the north-west corner of the churchyard.

Leave the churchyard at its north-east corner, the path dropping back down to the towpath of the canal. On the other side of the canal the timbered and picturesque Salwarpe Court can be glimpsed through the trees.

Following the towpath north-eastwards you soon hit modern times again in the form of the A38 which crosses the canal on a wide concrete span. You are now entering Droitwich town, but the canal stays in a green corridor right through.

After the second road bridge the undergrowth on the towpath will probably force you to join the tarmac path running parallel to the left alongside playing fields. This path rejoins the towpath which you continue to follow under more bridges, including a mini-tunnel under the railway.

You soon reach the wide canal basin which has been attractively landscaped to form a central park for the town. This is where the walk ends. A car park with toilets is on the far side of the road to the right. The main Worcester - Bromsgrove road is straight ahead, and the town centre is to the right.

14

Alrewas and Fradley Junction

by
Clive Hough

An easy but satisfying and interesting walk, just north of Lichfield, taking in two canals.

When James Brindley, the first great canal engineer, planned his Grand Trunk system of canals the residents of Fradley were not to know that one of the most important junctions on the canal system would be nearby. But it is here that the Coventry Canal, which links into the south-east waterways, meets the Trent and Mersey Canal. The junction is a focal point of this walk which starts at Alrewas.

> MAPS: Landranger 128
> Pathfinder 872 (SK01/11)
> CAR PARKING: Roadside in Alrewas
> BUS: Stevenson's 112 — Birmingham to Burton via Alrewas.
> START & FINISH: Alrewas (GR 170151)
> DISTANCE: 6 miles

Alrewas is a large homely village with many old buildings, including some fine timber framed cottages. Its unusual name derives from 'Alder Wash' which refers to the many alder trees that originally grew in the Trent valley — an area which was often flooded. The alders provided the raw materials for basket weaving for which the village was once famed.

Start in the main street, cross the canal bridge at the west end of the street and immediately turn right along Mill End Lane. You pass a school and the lane twists right to reach Alrewas church on your right. The church, which dates largely from the thirteenth and fourteenth centuries, has a broad nave with unmatched arches and an attractive churchyard.

Go through the churchyard, turn right and walk on along the road to the canal bridge. To the left is the River Trent, originally navigable when it served the old flour mill (probably soon to be converted into residences) that you can see behind you. Go down to the canal towpath and walk 500 yds north to the lock. This is where the Trent & Mersey Canal joins the River Trent to share its course for a few hundred yards.

Look out for the several watercourses hereabouts — a little further on a bridge crosses one of these.

Retrace your steps to the road bridge, passing on your way one of the original Trent and Mersey Canal mile-posts dated 1819 and continue south-west along the towpath, going through Bagnall Lock just outside

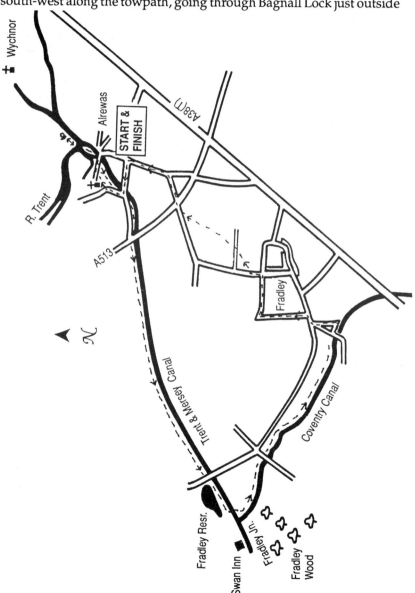

the village. After about a mile you pass the isolated Common Lock, surrounded by the level meadows of the Trent flood-plain. Over to the south-west you can see the high ground of Cannock Chase.

Continuing on, going past two more locks and a road bridge, you arrive at Fradley Junction and another lock. The Swan Inn here serves meals and bar snacks.

Cross the canal and walk up to where the Coventry Canal comes in from the left beside the fine Wharf House. Look across at the imposing row of canal cottages on the far side.

After lingering awhile at this peaceful canal-side settlement walk along the Coventry Canal, now going south-east. You go under New Bridge, then a former airfield occupies the right hand bank. The *Ladies of the Vale*, the three spires of Lichfield Cathedral, are visible beyond. Just over a mile from Fradley Junction you arrive at Fradley bridge.

About a hundred yards beyond the bridge go through a wicket gate to the left of two cottages and follow the access road to a white gate on the right. Go through here and across the field to another gate. Pass a cottage on your right, turn right and then first left at the Victorian church with a slim spire and ringed by yews. Follow the lane round a sharp right hand bend to a crossroads, turn left and climb the right hand fence to follow a field-path across the meadow to join a lane left of a cottage.

Enter the field opposite and follow the right hand edge to cross a bridge over

Milepost on the Trent & Mersey Canal

a stream and two stiles to reach a lane. Turn right and follow the lane to the A513. Cross this, go through a wicket gate opposite and along the road ahead. A left turn will then bring you back to the main street of Alrewas. The bus stop is outside the George & Dragon to the left, but before leaving the village do go right to look at the fine timber framed cottages a little way down the main street.

15
Handsacre to Whittington
by
Heinke Jenkins

A ramble through the Staffordshire countryside along the Trent and Mersey and the Coventry canals.

MAPS: Landranger 128
Pathfinder 872 (SK01/11), 892 (SK00/10)
CAR PARKING: Lichfield. Roadside parking in Handsacre
BUSES: Midland Red North. Service 825, Tamworth to Stafford via Handsacre, Lichfield and Whittington
START: Handsacre (GR 092162)
FINISH: Whittington (GR 163084)
DISTANCE: 9 miles

From Handsacre Village walk along The Green, pass the Crown Inn and cross the bridge over the Trent & Mersey canal. Turn right along the towpath. After a few hundred yards you will pass a canal mile-post — one of a number of replicas of the original mile-posts which were erected by the Trent & Mersey Canal Society in 1977. You will meet several of these on your walk, and also some of the originals which fortunately still survive.

Just past bridge 57 you leave the houses behind you and are now in the gentle Staffordshire countryside. The towpath is nicely tree lined, with many oaks, and remains so for quite a distance. After passing under the power transmission lines, taking electricity from the nearby Rugeley Power Station, you get a good view, over to the south-west, of the wooded hills of Cannock Chase.

Rugeley Power Station makes use of locally mined coal and this area is honeycombed with both old and new mine workings. This results in considerable subsidence and you will see several pools near to the canal which have most likely been formed in this way. A regular check is kept on the canal to see that it is not itself affected.

About 50 yards past the transmission lines the canal crosses the Bourne Brook by an aqueduct.

After going under the A515 Ravenshaw Wood is on the opposite bank.

Past the wood a row of stone blocks on the canal edge indicates that you are passing over a weir carrying overflow water from the canal into the ditch which you can see on your left.

Woodend Lock, which you soon meet, is particularly attractive with a fine canal cottage, originally the residence of the lock keeper. The row of planks on the left 'stop planks': these can be dropped into the slots that you can see by the top gate of the lock, thereby 'stopping off' a section of canal when this has to be drained for repairs. The purpose of the iron reinforcement bars on the bridge is to protect the brickwork from the continual passage of the tow-ropes of horse-drawn boats, now, unfortunately, a rarity on the canals. You can see how the iron has been worn away in places by the tow-ropes.

Woodend Lock marks the start of a gradual descent of the canal to the River Trent (see walk no. 14).

Past the lock you get a good view, over to the right, of the three spires of Lichfield Cathedral (the 'Ladies of the Vale'). Then, a few hundred

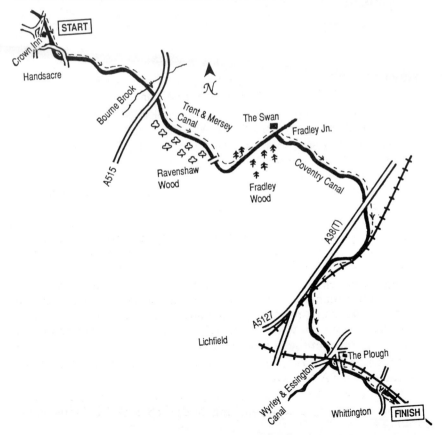

Fradley Junction

yards past the lock, you will find one of the original Trent & Mersey mile-posts dated 1819 and still in fine condition.

As the canal swings round to the left the buildings of a disused airfield can be seen on the edge of Fradley Wood.

After passing Shade House Lock and Middle Lock you come to Fradley Junction, the terminus of the Coventry Canal, completed in 1790. A signpost here, erected by the Coventry Canal Society, directs boats to Great Haywood, Shardlow and Coventry. 'The Swan' is adjacent and provides meals and bar snacks.

A few yards on you meet Junction Lock. Cross the canal here by the bridge and turn right to reach the towpath of the Coventry Canal. As you do so you pass the attractive and unspoiled Wharf House. The origin of this house is uncertain but it pre-dates the canal. When the canal came through it was made into three cottages for canal employees, then later converted to a residence and administrative offices for the engineer of the Coventry Canal. The garage of Wharf House is about 150 years old and was originally built as a boatmen's mission, some time later being converted into stables for canal horses.

At bridge 89 the towpath takes you under Icknield Street, the Roman Road now the A38. You can see how the bridge has been widened over the years as the road capacity has been increased.

About 200 yds before reaching bridge 88 a South Staffs Water

Company pumping station, dated 1891, can be seen over on the left. The railway now accompanies the canal for a short distance.

The sound of traffic racing along the A38 announces your return to Icknield Street which runs parallel with the canal for about half a mile. About 200 yds before reaching bridge 84 look out for a somewhat anonymous milestone in the grass beside the towpath announcing simply 2 and 3½ — obviously 2 miles to Whittington and 3½ miles from Fradley Junction.

Just past bridge 83 there is access to the garden of a pub, The Plough. Then, after passing under the railway, an abandoned section of the Wyrley and Essington Canal branches off to the right.

Leave the canal at bridge 80. Go up to the road, cross the canal and walk along the Burton Road into Whittington. The road swings round to the right to reach a crossroads and the Bell Inn. The bus stop for Lichfield and Handsacre is just outside the inn.

Woodend Lock on the Trent & Mersey Canal

16

In Search of Salt
by
Tony Watson

This circular walk starts at Shugborough Park and takes us to the village of Salt where we can visit an 800 year old inn. On the outward journey we pass some attractive pools and, on the way back, go along a section of the Trent and Mersey Canal which is accompanied by the winding River Trent.

N.B. The outward journey will take about four hours walking so, if you want to have lunch at the inn, an early start is necessary.

MAPS: Landranger 127
Pathfinder 850 (SJ82/92)
CAR PARKING: On A513, about 4½ miles east of Stafford.
BUSES: Midland Red North 823 and 825: Tamworth - Lichfield - Shugborough - Stafford.
RAILWAY STATIONS: Tamworth. Lichfield. Stafford.
START & FINISH: Shugborough Park (GR 988213)
DISTANCE: 12 miles

From the A513 enter Shugborough Park by one of the two entrances at White Barn Farm. As the road bends round to the left you can see to your left one of the seven unusual monuments that are a feature of the park. This one is the Triumphal Arch, a copy of Hadrian's Arch in Athens. On your right you will see a concreted channel carrying a stream. This is the old mill stream: it crosses the railway by an aqueduct, cascades down a few feet and then runs under the road into the mill pond, flanked by the old mill, which you will soon see on the left.

Follow the road past Shugborough Park Farm, the 'living museum' which is open from Easter to Christmas. Just past the farm on the left is a two storied octagonal building, another of the seven monuments. This is the Tower of the Winds, a copy of the Horologium in Athens. Do not follow the road in front of the Hall but continue in a straight line, passing through a small gate between two 'Except for Access' signs. Across to the left you have a fine view of Shugborough Hall, the ancestral home of Lord Lichfield. This fine mansion house, dating back to 1693, is now owned by the National Trust.

The track leads to Essex Bridge, an old pack-horse bridge which crosses the River Trent just below its confluence with the River Sow. It was built by the Earl of Essex in the seventeenth century as a shortcut to Cannock Chase. Originally possessing forty arches, it now has only fourteen — but it is still the longest pack-horse bridge in England.

Immediately before crossing the bridge over the Trent and Mersey Canal take the access, to the right, onto the canal towpath. Turn left under the bridge, following the canal past Haywood Lock. Continue along the towpath past the line of moored boats, and cross the Staffordshire and Worcestershire Canal at Haywood Bridge (No. 109). As you cross you will see, a little way along the canal to your left, an old toll house where tolls were levied on boats entering from the Trent and Mersey. You then meet the Anglo-Welsh boat-yard and a sign showing *Wolverhampton, The Potteries* and *The Trent*.

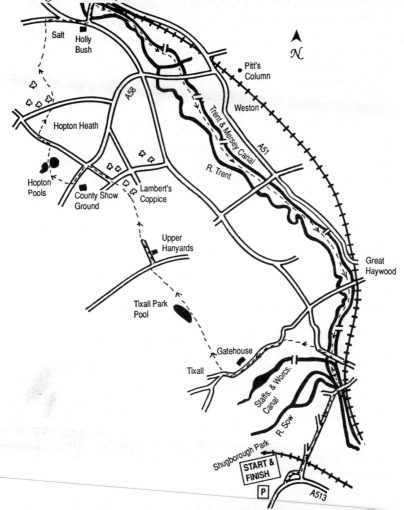

Immediately after the boat-yard, and before passing under the road bridge (No. 74), leave the towpath and turn left along the road, soon re-crossing the River Trent. Just past the river take the bridleway on the left by the side of a house and signposted Tixall. Cross the fields, keeping a hedge or a fence on your right. On meeting a fenced track continue in a straight line to Tixall Farm. As you head towards the farm you will see the Staffordshire and Worcestershire Canal as it runs along an embankment to your left.

The Essex bridge, Shugborough

Approaching the impressive, stone built, Tixall Farm you will see an old toll house. Turn left by it and follow the road for about half a mile (watching carefully for the traffic) until you reach the village of Tixall. As you walk along the road look across to the 'Broad Water' (also known as the 'Tixall Wide') to your left. The canal opens out here to create the impression of a lake when viewed from the now vanished Tixall Hall.

The first Tixall Hall was built in 1555 by Sir Edward Aston — Mary, Queen of Scots, was held prisoner here for seventeen days in 1586. The old hall was demolished and a new hall built during the period 1750 to 1787, but this, in turn, was demolished in 1927. However, the fine Tudor Gate-house of the Hall, built around 1575, still remains and you will soon pass this on your right.

Opposite St. John the Baptist Church, in Tixall, turn right off the main road by the cottages and the telephone box, following the private road to Tixall Mews. The road crosses a bridge (Dairy Bridge) over a now overgrown estate pathway. The stone bridge is particularly handsome and is a Grade 2 listed structure. It probably dates from the eighteenth century when the second hall was built. On the far right side it is inscribed HIC VER PERPETUUM (Here is perpetual Spring). The origin of this is obscure but it seems most probable that the pathway originally led through a landscaped area, providing an attractive walk, or ride, for the occupants of Tixall Hall.

As the road veers off to the right, just past the bridge, take the large gate to your left into a field (not the small gate just beyond). Follow the line of the hedge and the dyke on your right and when the dyke ends in a pond continue in the same line directly up the hill, under the electricity pylons, until you reach the corner of the field and the fence around Square Covert. Take a minute here to look back and admire the view of Cannock Chase.

Go through the gate and head half left for the corner of the fence around Tixall Park Pool, an attractive expanse of water formed by damming a small stream, popular with Canada Geese and other water fowl. From the corner of the fence the right of way now angles slightly away from the pool heading to just short of the top left hand corner of the field where you will meet a track coming up from the left. Go through the gap in the hedge on the left of the track beside an oak and follow the fence to your left. Cross the field, leaving it by a wicket gate just to the right of the far left hand corner of the field. Go straight through a small field, leaving it through a gate onto a lane. Turn right, then left to Upper Hanyards Farm. The track passes through the farmyard and leaves via two gates to a grassy track. To your left you will catch a glimpse of Stafford.

The track heads towards a small pool, but the right of way, unfortunately, does not extend as far as this. When the track starts to swing left go through a gate on the right and go diagonally across the field, heading for the corner of the wood which you can see ahead. This will bring you to a fine stone wall which surrounds Lambert's Coppice. Turn left, go through a wicket gate and walk alongside this wall.

The path leads to a surfaced driveway coming from Deer Park Farm. Continue along the driveway to reach the A518. Here turn left and walk about 200 yards along the grass verge, passing a Hopton and Coton Parish milestone, to reach an entrance to the Staffordshire County Show Ground. Cross the road here and go over a stile to a footpath signposted Hopton Pools. Follow the path with the fence on your right to a second stile from where you will see one of the two pools ahead of you. Head for the left side of this pool to reach a stile. Cross this and follow the path, passing between the two pools, then through Hopton Pools Covert and a field to the road. Climb the stile and turn left along the road which runs in front of RAF, Stafford.

As the road bends round to the right you will find a stile on your right.

Holly Bush Inn, the second oldest inn in England

Cross this into a field which was the site of the 'Battle of Hopton Heath', an inconclusive Civil War battle which took place on 19 March 1643. After passing down the side of the RAF station cross a stile, follow the field path with the hedge on your left and go through a gate to Brick Kiln Covert. Ignore the track which immediately goes off sharply to the left but go forward a few yards and take the left fork through the deciduous wood to a gate. Cross the field to the gate opposite and enter the coniferous Salt Heath. Follow the main track until, just after passing a fenced pheasant compound, you meet a path coming in from a stile on your right. Turn left onto this path and continue to a stile into a field. From here follow the track down the hill, keeping a fence on your right, until the track swings off to the right through a gate. At this point go ahead between four trees and then half right down the field to cross a stile. Go forward with the fence on your right, cross two stiles and then go between two hedges to meet the road on the outskirts of the village of Salt.

Turn right and follow the road through the village, passing the church of St. James the Great and a very attractive row of old cottages on the left. Towards the end of the village you meet the thatched Holly Bush Inn (restaurant and bar snacks). Dating from 1190, and reputedly the second oldest inn in England, it was licensed by James I in 1610. The inn was a stopping point for the mule and pony trains coming with salt from nearby Shirleywich on their way to Stafford.

Just past the Holly Bush take the road to the left, crossing the River

Trent to reach the Trent and Mersey Canal. Immediately before the canal bridge, with its fine brickwork, turn right onto the canal towpath. The meandering River Trent, to the right, will now accompany us back to Essex Bridge. To your left you will see the 75 ft. high Pitt's Column, erected as a tribute to the eighteenth century Prime Minister which stands in Sandon Park.

You will soon pass a Trent and Mersey Canal mile-post. Although this is one of many reproductions erected by the Trent and Mersey Canal Society you will later meet two original ones dating from 1817. These mile-posts will enable you to time your progress along the towpath.

If you look across to the right just after the canal crosses a small stream you will see Weston Hall. Just after emerging from bridge 80 there is a beautiful row of cottages to the right, beside the Saracen's Head pub.

Continue along the grassy towpath, passing under Sandhill Bridge (No. 81) and through Weston and past Weston Lock.

Bridge over the Trent & Mersey Canal at Salt

At Ingestre Bridge (No. 78) you may be able to catch a glimpse through the trees of Ingestre Hall, about half a mile away along the road to the right. This was originally a Tudor building but was rebuilt in neo-Gothic style following a major fire in 1820.

At Hoo Mill Lock a busy boat-yard stretches to either side. At Haywood Bridge you are back to the earlier section of the walk. Again cross the Staffordshire and Worcestershire Canal, return to Haywood Lock and leave the canal at bridge 73. Head back across Essex Bridge and Shugborough Park to your starting point. But, if time permits, try to visit Shugborough Hall or the Farm Museum.

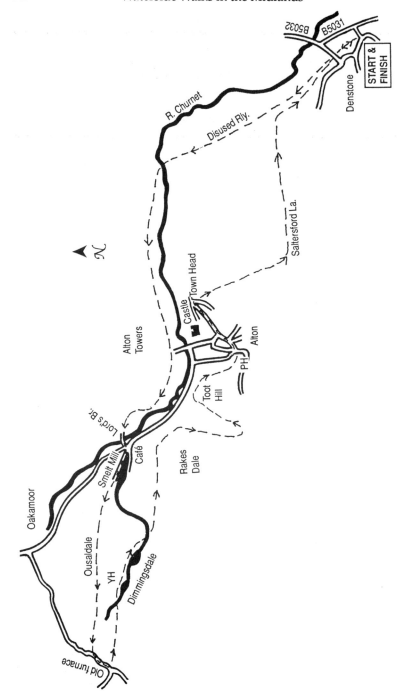

17

The Churnet Valley

by
Arthur Foden

This circular walk, much of it along the River Churnet near Alton in Staffordshire, explores also the delightful twin miniature valleys of Ousal and Dimmingsdale with the remains of an old smelting mill. We also visit Toothill, a prominent rocky outcrop and viewpoint overlooking the Churnet Valley.

MAPS: Landranger 119 and 128
Pathfinder 810 (SK04/14)
CAR PARK: By Denstone Village Hall.
BUSES: PMT 238/9 Uttoxeter - Cheadle via Denstone
Stevenson's 409 Uttoxeter - Ashbourne via Denstone.
RAILWAY STATION: Uttoxeter
START & FINISH: Denstone (Old railway station GR 101407)
DISTANCE: 10½ miles.

The walk starts from Denstone along the disused railway line which once passed through the village but has now been converted into an attractive public walkway with lots of plant and bird-life. The entrance will be found opposite the village post office.

Follow the line, keeping company with the River Churnet all the way to Alton (2 miles), crossing the river after about a mile. Approaching Alton the Castle stands out prominently high up on the left. Go under the road bridge and past the old station (now a private residence) continuing along the track.

The sound of rushing water will soon be heard as you approach the weir from where water was once diverted to drive an old mill close by. A little path on the left will take you to see the weir and give you a good view of the river. Shortly a bridge over the track comes into view, and at this point (approximately 100 yds. short of the bridge) you leave the old railway line via a footbridge over a ditch on your right.

Beyond, follow a path going left, soon joining a well defined track coming in from the right. Go left along this which brings you out onto the bridge crossing the old railway. A short distance further on you will pass over a second bridge (Lord's Bridge) spanning the River Churnet to reach a lane. Cross straight over this, passing to the right of the

Rambler's Retreat Café. Take the rightmost track, passing on the left the old smelting mill and a large pool adjoining it. Way-marks indicate that you are here on the Staffordshire Way, a ninety mile long-distance path across the county.

You are now entering Ousal Dale, a deeply wooded valley which, along with its neighbour, nearby Dimmingsdale, adds a special charm to this particular part of Staffordshire. The pool and surrounding area are especially attractive when the rhododendrons, of which there are many, are in flower. Halfway alongside the pool the track divides. You can take either branch as they rejoin further on. The right-hand one climbs at first but levels out where it swings sharply left, becoming a delightful high level promenade with several interesting rock outcrops.

When the paths unite again you climb a short way to reach a gate and open country. The signposted track going left here leads to The Ranger Youth Hostel. Follow the obvious route going straight ahead and over a cattle grid, still following the Staffordshire Way. This soon joins a farm track coming in from the left and eventually reaches a narrow lane. You are on high ground here with wide ranging views, especially northwards over Oakamoor.

Turn left down the lane and at the bottom of the hill, after passing some cottages on the left, you will reach a junction. Go left down the track signposted Dimmingsdale ¾ Alton 2. Water is a prominent feature here as you will soon realize when a small fast flowing stream crosses your path, with a little footbridge over it. A little further on, to the left, this natural flow of water has been utilised to form an artificial ornamental pond in which water loving plants are much in evidence.

The stream recrosses your path and a more substantial stream forms on the right. Shortly, the main track goes left to a gate. However, you should continue ahead alongside the stream, passing several small pools on the right and soon reaching the first of several attractive larger ones. Note here, over your left shoulder, the nearby circular building. After the second pool stay on the track which now crosses to the right.

Just before the track bends sharply left climb some stone steps on the right and take a narrow path which ascends the bank to a stile and open country. (N.B. Ignore an earlier path at a less sharp bend which leaves the track by wooden steps.)

Continue ahead from the stile and, when a cottage comes in view, head for a stile to the right of it. Looking across the valley here you can see parts of the Alton Towers amusement complex. Cross the stile and pass the cottage on your left to reach a track with a road and river below on the left. Follow this down to reach the road at a bend.

Here a signposted footpath climbs the steep wooded bank in front. Ignore this and turn instead onto a broad track going right up Rakes

Dale. When this forks take the left, slightly overgrown, track, soon reaching a stile. From here proceed up a narrow deep sided valley, with rocky outcrops on both sides, heading for a gate in front of a large stone house dated 1874. Do not go through the gate but follow the fence on the right a short distance to a stile which will enable you to cross to the drive beyond.

Follow the drive and then, at the top, double back sharply left onto a higher track alongside a stone wall. At first surfaced this soon becomes a lovely old green lane. On reaching a sharp bend leave the lane by a path between newly built dry-stone walls which leads to a National Trust sign and, beyond, Toothill Rock. This is a lofty viewpoint in the care of the National Trust, with far-reaching views up and down the valley and the river below. Across the valley Alton Flag Tower stands out, while perched high on the right Alton Castle is seen at its best.

Dimmingsdale Pools

Now retrace your steps to the green lane and follow this to the Royal Oak public house on the outskirts of Alton. Take the road opposite, which climbs, and at the top go left, noting here the round structure on the right which was the old lock-up. A little further on, at a junction, go right along High Street passing several inns, the church and a close-up of the Castle Tower on the left.

High Street leads into Town Head — continue to the end of this road and turn the corner to the right into Hurstons Lane where you will find a stile in the fence on your left. We have now rejoined the Staffordshire Way and our path is waymarked. Head half left across the field to a stile in the top left corner, then beyond follow the hedge on the left over two fields to reach a green lane (Saltersford Lane). Turn left and follow this, finding a single line of paving blocks, some quite old, for almost its whole length (¾ mile). Saltersford Lane is an old 'salt road' along which salt was brought by mule train from Cheshire. The stone blocks by the side of the paving probably marked the parish boundary. The lane can be very muddy in wet weather.

When the double hedgerow finishes continue to follow a hedge on the right to a stile. Cross this and continue alongside the hedge until this turns sharp right, then head straight across the field to a Staffordshire Way signpost alongside the hedge on the far side. Turn right, following the hedgerow now on your left. Continue across several fields with the disused railway and river across to the left. On reaching a stile with a ladder approach, which leads up to the B5032, ignore this and pass instead through a convenient gap in the hedge on the left to regain the old railway line. You now have only a short distance to go to your starting point in Denstone.

18

A Potteries Round

by
John Smith

A circular walk which explores some of the industrial heritage of Stoke-on-Trent but which stays 'green' for most of the way.

> MAPS: Landranger 118
> Pathfinder 809 (SJ84/94), 792 (SJ85/95)
> Street plan of Stoke-on-Trent
> CAR PARKS: Longport Station, Westport Water Park
> BUSES: PMT 92 Newcastle - Burslem - Endon; 94 Newcastle - Burslem - Chell Heath;
> 98 Newcastle - Turnstall - Biddulph
> RAILWAY STATION: Longport
> START & FINISH: Longport (GR 856494)
> DISTANCE: 9 miles

From Longport station walk the 300 yards up Station Street to Newcastle Street and the Trent and Mersey Canal bridge. The entrance to the canal is opposite the Duke of Bridgewater pub.

This is an appropriate start to our walk, for it was the Duke of Bridgewater who employed James Brindley to build a canal, opened in 1761, to serve the coal mines owned by the Duke in Worsley, near Manchester. Brindley, a self taught engineer, subsequently went on to build many of the major early canals. Opposite the Duke of Bridgewater is another pub, the Packhorse. This too is an appropriate name — packhorse trains were the earlier means of conveying goods that were replaced by the much more efficient canals.

Join the towpath to the left, have a quick look at the bottle oven opposite (one of several that we shall meet on our walk), then turn right and duck under the low bridge. Now follow the towpath for two miles to the bridge at Etruria Road (A53).

For the first mile the left bank of the canal is lined with old pottery factories, now interspersed with green areas, and one or two old bottle ovens can still be seen. We pass two canal cranes at former canal wharfs, the first now a car park. The former importance of the canal system to the Potteries is very apparent. The second mile sees a change to steel as the rolling mills and warehouses of British Steel take over the right bank.

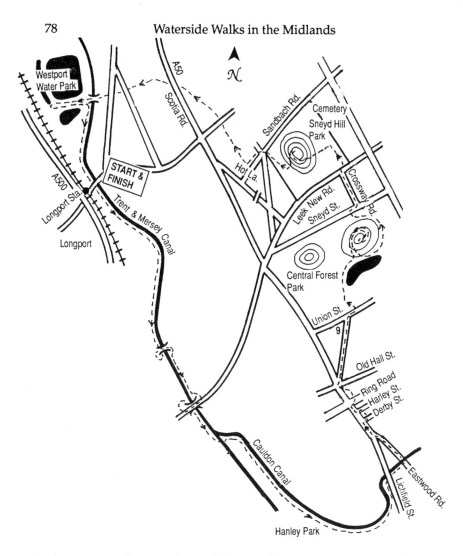

A quarter mile or so beyond the Middleport Pottery building is a path-side seat in front of a length of old retaining wall. This wall is built from sagger bottoms. Saggers were containers used to hold the ware while it was being fired in the bottle ovens.

Approaching a road bridge observe that the service road to the right is, in places, surfaced with broken pottery, some of it nicely decorated Wedgwood. Just past the bridge you pass a canal mile-post of traditional design, recently erected by the Trent and Mersey Canal Society.

After passing under a bridge of an abandoned railway a pleasantly landscaped area can be seen on the opposite bank, which includes an artificial ski slope. This was part of the area that was regenerated for the Garden Festival of 1986. Prior to the festival all this land, from the canal almost to the centre of Hanley, was owned by British Steel. Known locally as Shelton Bar, this steelmaking plant closed in 1978 leaving only the rolling mills now remaining on the other side of the canal.

After going over a canal weir the towpath crosses to the other side. See the grooves in the ironwork of the bridge — these were cut by the passage, over many years, of the tow-ropes.

When meeting a steel stockyard we cross a bridge over what remains of an arm of the canal. The stables that you can see here were not, as you might think, for canal horses but were constructed, together with other buildings and a narrow gauge tramway, to simulate an old coal mine for the Garden Festival. From the bridge you have a good view of Josiah Wedgwood's home, Etruria Hall. This escaped demolition by the steelmakers because they used it as offices.

An old bottle oven beside the Trent & Mersey Canal

Just past the China Garden inn a lift bridge takes us over the entrance to a marina, also created for the 1986 Gardens Festival.

After passing the marina the towpath changes sides again, so go up the ramp to Etruria Road, cross the canal, and descend past the Roundhouse. This is all that remains of the original Wedgwood factory — and the original reason for building it is now forgotten! As a board beside the towpath explains, the Roundhouse houses an exhibition of old printing equipment belonging to the Evening Sentinel newspaper company — but this exhibition is, unfortunately, not open to the general public.

Go back under the road and on to the summit lock. At this point the Caldon Canal branches off to the left while the Trent and Mersey Canal continues down the locks to Stoke. James Brindley, whose statue here was unveiled in July 1990, was employed by Josiah Wedgwood to link the rivers Trent and Mersey by a canal opened in 1777. Follow the Trent and Mersey Canal for 100 yds to the next lock and have a look at the old Etruscan Bone and Flint Mill, erected 1857 and now the Etruria Industrial Museum, where the raw materials for making bone china were once ground. Return to the top lock and cross the Trent and Mersey Canal to reach the Caldon Canal opened in 1779, noting, at the junction, the dry dock. We now follow the Caldon Canal for a mile and a half to Lichfield Street (A50).

Shortly after leaving the junction we meet two locks comprising a 'staircase' — here the top gates of the lower lock constitute the bottom gates of the higher lock, a characteristic feature found when a canal has to navigate a steep gradient.

At the next lock note the 'split bridge', the split in the centre allowing the tow-rope to pass through.

The emphasis now reverts to pottery and we pass a mixture of potteries, glaze and colour mills, and houses. Then follows a very quiet stretch where the canal passes through Hanley Park.

After leaving the park and swinging northwards the path overlooks the valley of the hidden River Trent for a short while before passing under Lichfield Street. Here large pottery factories appear on both sides and the canal is still used to transport pottery for a short distance. The boats used, one a catamaran, the Milton Maid, can usually be seen tied to the far bank.

Continue to the next bridge over the canal. Leave the towpath here and turn left up Eastwood Road noting the old houses, built as close as possible to the factory, and Stubbs Lane, still cobbled, on the right. At the top, cross Derby Street and continue straight ahead up an alley by a car park to Harley Street. Turn left at the concrete bollards, then immediately right to resume your line up to the ring road. Cross this at the crossing and continue straight ahead to join Lichfield Street just short of its junction with Old Hall Street at The Albion public house.

At this point, if you look left, you will see Hanley Town Hall. Stoke-on-Trent has seven town halls, one for each town except Burslem which has two. This is because the people of Burslem were so confident that Burslem would become the administrative centre of the proposed federation of the six towns that they had a new bigger hall built in readiness. They must have been quite upset when Stoke-upon-Trent got the job and the city of Stoke-on-Trent was formed!

Our route now passes right through the centre of Hanley. Cross Old Hall Street into Tontine Street. Pass the Post Office and at the end bear slightly right into Parliament Row (where stands a statue to Sir Stanley Matthews who was born in Hanley) to the top of the Market Square. Here you see the new red brick Potteries Shopping Centre. Keep this on your left and continue up Town Road to Quadrant Road. Cross Quadrant Road, go through a pleasant seating area marked by five stones and continue along the paved way with a multistorey car park, also brick built, on your left. Continue over the bridge, which crosses the ring road, to Union Street. Cross Union Street and turn half right to where a large mine wheel set in a concrete plinth marks a path to the left .

Just past the wheel the path forks. Take the right fork and then, at the third group of seats, leave the main track and go left between trees, heading for the lake which you can see ahead. Walk round the far side of the lake passing a grassed area between the two hills. As the path starts to swing right take the path which angles back sharply left and ascends the rightmost hill. Continue to the summit for some fine views of the surrounding area, an orientation point enabling you to locate many areas of interest. On a clear day you can see the Pennines to the north-east.

The shops are now half a mile behind and have been replaced by more relics of former industry, this time coal mining. We are now in the Central Forest Park which occupies the site of the old Hanley Deep Pit. The large wheel was a headgear pulley, and the two hills were spoil-heaps. To the north can be seen the spoil-heaps of two other collieries — Sneyd, our next objective, and Chatterley Whitfield which is now a museum.

Return to the lake and take the path which continues round the hill. Where it forks, go right, still circling round the hill, until you reach an open grassed area. Cross this diagonally and go between fences to reach Sneyd Street. Turn right for a hundred yards, then left into Crossway Road which leads to Leek New Road (A53). Cross this and just to the right enter Sneyd Hill Park. A path to the right, then to the left, leads to the top of the hill from where you have good view over Burslem and Tunstall.

Retrace your steps until you reach a wooden bridge over a gulley. Cross this and follow the gulley steeply down for thirty yards, then turn right. This will bring you to Sandbach Road at its junction with Hot Lane and Nevada Lane. Cross Sandbach Road and go down Hot Lane to the right of the garage. At the railway bridge turn right and go up the slope to join the Burslem Greenway. Go straight ahead in a north-westerly direction. Pass under four bridges (now converted into short tunnels) to where a new leisure centre marks the crossing of Scotia Road (A50).

The pottery industry developed in Stoke-on-Trent because both clay and coal were available. However, the transport system in the early days was very poor and so the potters, with Josiah Wedgwood as treasurer, had the canals built. These were eventually superseded by the railways and the path that we are now on was originally the Potteries Loop Line. It left the main line from Stoke to Crewe at Etruria, and looped through Hanley, Burslem and Tunstall before rejoining the main line at Kidsgrove. It was itself superseded by roads in the Beeching era.

Cross Scotia Road and follow the path for a further hundred yards to where a side track joins from the left. Follow this past some old buffers and under two bridges to a road which leads into Westport Water Park.

The Fowlea Brook Nature Reserve

The path has now left the Loop Line and follows the old mineral line which was used for the movement of coal. Two different branches of the pottery industry can be seen to the right of this path. Before the bridges is a large tile works, and beyond is a brickworks.

Westport Water Park is a complex of lakes between the canal and the Stoke - Crewe railway, and is the home to a large number of birds, especially during the winter months. Like the two parks that we met earlier it was made on derelict industrial ground.

Westport, Longport and Middleport are strange names to find fifty miles from the sea. But these were the canal ports for the early potteries, and from here their wares were shipped around the world via the canals to Liverpool. Port Vale Football Club also originated in and took its name from this area. Swans, coots and gulls now occupy its old pitch.

Take time to explore the lakes, especially the hidden ones in a nature reserve area by the Fowlea Brook. You will discover these by walking clockwise about a quarter of the way around the larger lake and then crossing a stile on the left. Then return to the canal and turn right under the bridge (south). Note the unglazed teapots that you can see through the windows of the factory that you soon pass opposite, then walk the quarter mile to the bottle oven which was the start, and is now the end, of our walk.

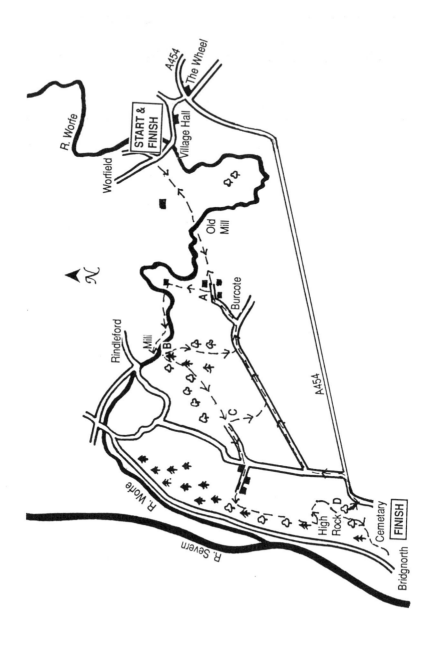

19
Worfield And the River Worfe
by
Arthur Foden

This is a walk with several variations which will introduce you to the delights of the River Worfe, one of Shropshire's minor rivers. It flows through some very attractive countryside in its short life and has the added attraction of two old water-wheels. You also have the opportunity to visit High Rock, a prominent viewpoint overlooking the Worfe's more noted neighbour, the River Severn.

MAPS: Landranger 138
Pathfinder 911 (SO69/79)
CAR PARK: Near to Worfield Village Hall
BUS: Midland Red North, Wolverhampton - Bridgnorth via Worfield
START: Worfield (GR 757954)
FINISH: Worfield (GR 757954) or Bridgnorth (GR 724934)
DISTANCES: Worfield circuits A-B-A 4 miles; A-B-C-A 4½miles; A-B-C-D-A 6½miles
Worfield - Bridgnorth 4½miles

The walk starts on the edge of Worfield village. To reach this leave the A454 Wolverhampton - Bridgnorth road, approximately 3½ miles north-east of Bridgnorth at the cross roads signposted Worfield (GR 764953) opposite The Wheel public house (where the Wolverhampton - Bridgnorth bus will drop you). After crossing a stream go left at a road junction. At the first building (the Village Hall), a short distance from the junction, limited car parking is available.

From the Village Hall walk along the lane to the outskirts of the village to another road junction (GR 757954). The road going to the right is a loop road into the village only, but this is worth exploring if you have the time.

On the left, opposite the junction, is the entrance to the grounds of Davenport House and to the left of this a stile, the starting point for this walk. Cross this, then follow the fence on the right, shortly reaching a stile in it. Proceed across the middle of the field beyond, using a tree in the centre as a guide to reach another stile which gives access onto the drive of Davenport House. Go straight over the drive and climb the steep bank opposite to reach a way-mark post on top. Continue forward and cross again the same drive which circles the hillside in a loop. Go ahead on a track which descends a shallow valley. Follow this to reach a gateway. Cross the pasture ahead, making for a clump of trees, passing to the left of a large isolated tree as you do so.

This will bring you to a footbridge over the River Worfe where you can see the remains of a large water-wheel and its attendant pumping gear. Swing right over the bridge, following the river and soon passing an air vent with the sound of running water below: this apparently has some connection with the water-wheel.

The field now narrows: at the end of it climb the stile alongside a gate and follow the track across the next field making for some buildings. On reaching these pass through a gate between a barn and the corner of a cottage garden. This brings you out onto a well defined path via a waymarked stile. (Burcote. Map, point **A**)

Turn right onto this path (even though the way-mark suggests

Old water wheel on the River Worfe
Photo Bob Jones

going left), passing behind the cottage. This section is wooded and the river can be seen below on the right. On leaving the trees at a stile a low sandstone cliff appears on the left. The path follows this until, at the end of it, you turn a corner to be confronted by a house. A broad fenced track through the trees on the left passes around the buildings, coming out onto a drive beyond. Go forward along this drive which soon crosses the river and continues down an attractive wooded valley to the hamlet of Rindleford by the old mill

On reaching the gate just before the mill go forward and then turn left, passing between the mill on your right and a nursery garden on your left. Do not be mislead by various PRIVATE notices displayed here as it is a right of way. This leads to another footbridge over the river — note here the old mill-wheel behind the mill. A second footbridge, spanning an overflow channel, brings you out via a stile onto a well defined track on the opposite side of the river and heading back upstream.

Another sandstone cliff soon appears on the right and shortly, at a break in this, a valley goes off to the right. (Point **B**)

You now have a choice of four routes:

Route 1. A short circular route returning to Worfield.

Route 2. A slightly longer circular route to Worfield.

Route 3. Two miles longer than Route 2, this circular route to Worfield includes the superb viewpoint of High Rock.

Route 4. Worfield to Bridgnorth.

Route 1. Continue alongside the river on a clear track which soon climbs gently, leaving the river to reach a lane. The woods on this section are a mass of bluebells in the spring. On reaching the lane go left and in approximately ¼ mile turn left down the farm drive to Burcote House.

At the farm buildings follow a broad track which by-passes them to the left. This leads to the cottage that you met on the outward journey (Point **A**) and it only remains to retrace your steps back to Worfield.

Route 2. Leave the river (point **B**) to follow the floor of this valley (there is plenty of bird and plant life to be seen). The path soon merges with a forest track coming in from the left which, at this point, becomes partly surfaced with granite chippings. Continue forward along this until you reach a gate at the head of the valley (The Batch, point **C**).

You can now return to Worfield by turning left beyond this gate to another gate, on the right of which is the remains of a stile. A path traverses an area of rough heathland leading to a stile, beyond which is a small valley. Walk up the centre of this and at the head of the valley, just beyond a small corrugated iron shed, swing left to a gate leading out onto a lane. Turn left along this and after approximately ¼ mile you reach the farm drive to Burcote House. From here follow the directions given in the last paragraph of Route 1.

Route 3. Proceed as described in the first paragraph of Route 2 to the gate at point **C**. Now continue ahead at this gate until you reach a lane, then cross straight over to a track opposite. Pass a cottage on your right, then two more buildings on the left. The track narrows before reaching an old gateway, beyond which the ground suddenly drops away steeply in front.

Turn left through the gateway, following a narrow path on the top of a wooded bank. Ignore a path which shortly descends right and continue on the high ground with an open field on the left. Care is required on this section, especially after rain or snow. On reaching the corner of the field on the left the woods open out and you continue ahead on an easier path, which soon forks. Go right here to reach High Rock, a lofty viewpoint overlooking the River Severn at Bridgnorth.

You can now continue forward on the path, although this will involve clambering down some rocks a short way ahead (not very difficult). To avoid this return to the fork and turn right.

You now descend a series of sandstone steps. At the bottom of one flight of these the path swings sharp left. However, before doing this a short diversion to the right leads to the best viewpoint.

On swinging left the path goes in a loop through woodland, circling round the head of a valley. There is plenty of bird life here. On reaching the other side of the valley you meet a path running alongside a field. Turn right along this path and, at a corner of the field, another path can be seen which descends steeply right (Point **D**).

If you want to go on to Bridgnorth now follow the instructions for route 4. However, to return to Worfield, keep left here on the higher path which continues just inside the tree-line, soon reaching the A454. Go left along this and then shortly take the first lane on the left, then first right until reaching the drive to Burcote. From here continue as described in the last two sentences of Route 1.

Route 4. Follow the instructions for Route 3 up to point **D**. Then go down the path which descends right through a rocky gulley to cross a stile at the edge of the wood. Continue ahead on high ground soon reaching a sandstone wall on the left which surrounds a cemetery. Continue to the end of the wall and a stile, cross this and descend the enclosed path, still alongside the cemetery wall, arriving at the bottom at the cemetery entrance. Turn right for the A442, then left for the centre of Bridgnorth, looking out for some fine stone cottages and timber framed buildings as you enter the town.

20
Streams of the Long Mynd
by
Derek and Maureen Field

This circular walk follows the course of two streams which drain the Long Mynd, one of the jewels of the Shropshire Hills. The walk is rough going in places and sturdy footwear is essential. Make sure you have good waterproofs and warm clothing if the weather is likely to be bad.

MAPS: Landranger 137
Pathfinder 910 (SO49/59)
PARKING: Roadside in Little Stretton. On the Portway at Pole Cottage In Church Stretton.
RAILWAY STATION: Church Stretton (1½ m)
START AND FINISH: Little Stretton (GR 443917) or Church Stretton (GR 453938)
DISTANCE: 6½ miles (or 9½ miles if starting from Church Stretton)

Our walk starts at the Ragleth Arms in Little Stretton which lies to the south of Church Stretton on the B4370. *If you prefer to begin in Church Stretton go into the centre of the town and walk south along the B4370. Little Stretton is about 1½ miles along this quiet and pleasant road. If you prefer to start from the car park on the Portway continue reading from the point marked ➦ on p. 91.*

On the opposite corner of the crossroads to the Ragleth Arms is a pretty black and white church, dating only from 1903 but one of the very few churches in England to have a thatched roof. It is worth spending a few minutes looking at this before setting out.

Take the lane which runs beside the Ragleth Arms, turn left at the T-junction, pass an attractive timber framed cottage on the right, then fork right at the farm. Follow this lane for about half a mile and cross a stream. About 300 yards after crossing the stream a track leads into a conifer wood. Turn right and walk into the wood. After a few yards turn right again at the sign for Callow Hollow. The path follows a fence round the edge of the wood until a stile is reached. Cross the stile, turn right and follow the path down to the stream. Turn left alongside this. You are now in Callow Hollow.

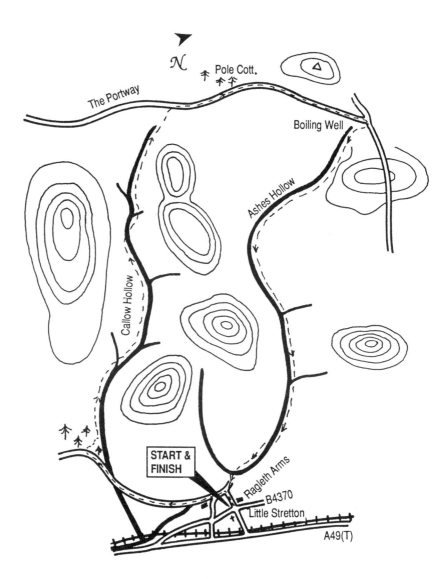

The walk now follows the course of the stream, the rough path criss-crossing from one bank to the other. There are many small pools and fish can be seen in the crystal clear water.

Eventually the stream disappears altogether. Continue walking uphill and you will very shortly reach a surfaced road; a fence runs along the other side of the road at this point. This road is the Portway and it runs along the crest of the Long Mynd. It was a trading route for Neolithic axe-traders and was recognised as a King's Highway in the Middle Ages, being used by Welsh drovers taking cattle to Shrewsbury market. From here on a good day you will probably see gliders from the Midland Gliding Club, about a mile to the south.

Thatched church at Little Stretton

Turn right and walk along the Portway. From here there are fine views of the surrounding Shropshire Hills: you might like to make a short diversion across to the trig point which marks the highest point on the Long Mynd (1696 ft).

➡ *Pole Cottage car park is about half a mile along the Portway if you prefer to start your walk from here.*

After walking about a mile along the Portway the road bends sharply to the right and there is a footpath sign to Little Stretton. The path down Ashes Hollow starts here to the left of the boggy patch called Boiling Well, which is where the stream rises that we are about to follow. The path is well defined, going sometimes to the left of the stream, sometimes to the right. At the bottom cross a footbridge at the farm and go through two fields to reach a track, the second field being a camp site.

Turn left along the track, then go right over a footbridge. The track swings right, now becoming surfaced. When you reach the fork turn left to return to the Ragleth Arms at Little Stretton.

Ashes Hollow

21

The Peaceful Dove
by
Heinke Jenkins

The Dove is well known to visitors in the popular area of Dovedale. In this walk we explore a less well known stretch of this charming river, visit the remains of an ancient abbey and discover some attractive Staffordshire villages and countryside.

MAPS: Landranger 128
Pathfinder 810 (SK04/14)
CAR PARKS: Roadside parking in Clifton.
BUS: Trent Service 107, Derby - Ashbourne. Then walk about one mile along the A515 to Clifton.
START & FINISH: Clifton (GR 165448)
DISTANCE: 9½miles

Leave your car near the church in Clifton. Walk back to the west side of the church and go down the steep road (about 100 yds to the left of the Cock Inn) signposted 'Mayfield 1¼'. At the old Station House turn left and walk along the tarmac road (once a railway, servicing a cotton mill) to Church Mayfield, crossing a stream and a bridge over the Henmore Brook, passing the old cotton mill (still working, but now spinning polyester) and the terraced mill workers' houses.

When you reach some blue factory gates turn left and then almost immediately right to cross a little bridge over the Dove. Pass some allotments and then more modern terraced houses with pretty gardens in a fenced lane. At the end of the lane turn left towards the church along a road passing more workers terraces.

Enter the churchyard and turn right where the path divides to go behind the church. Leave the churchyard by a gate and go north through three fields along a well-defined footpath towards Mayfield. After crossing a parking area, cross the B5032, then go straight on over a stile and through another field. The path swings slightly right to reach a stile. Continue forward across the next field aiming for a gate which is roughly midway between two tall trees that you can see ahead.

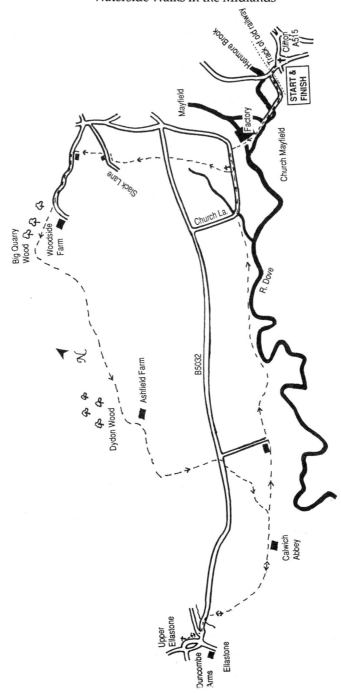

Cross the stile beside the gate and then bear slightly right to go diagonally across the next field. Cross another stile which is about twenty yards to the right of the bottom right-hand corner of the field. Keeping to the right of the hedge go about fifty yards through the next field and then left over a stile in the hedge onto Slack Lane.

Turn right in front of an electricity sub-station and then left to cross a stile beside the corner of the fence around the sub-station. Go uphill straight across the field ahead, then through a small second field past a farmhouse to emerge onto a lane and turn left along this.

Past a farm the lane loses its surfacing to become a farm track, now signed as a public footpath. Continue along this track until, just before reaching Woodside Farm, it swings sharply left. Just past the bend, leave the track on the right along a faintly defined path and go uphill aiming towards the rightmost of the two electricity posts that you can see ahead.

Swing right alongside the garden of Woodside Farm to reach, and cross, a stile on the left followed immediately by another stile. Go diagonally across the field and cross a ditch and a stile which you will find roughly in the centre of the hedge ahead. Cross the next field, aiming slightly to the left of the electricity post in the centre of the field, to reach a stone stile, also in roughly the centre of the hedge.

Turn left through a gate along a farm track. This leads you along the ridge for about two miles, soon giving fine views across to the west. After reaching a stile and a gate beside a small pond the track disappears. However, continue forward along the ridge, keeping to the right of a hedge and then, after going through a gate, to the left of a hedge.

After passing Ashfield Farm you are now on a good farm track. When this turns sharp left go through the gate opposite the bend in road. Continue forward across the field keeping to the left of some small trees, the remnants of an old hedge. Just past these cross a stone stile and a ditch which you will find to the right of an oak tree. Cross the next field diagonally to reach a gate. Go through this and then forward with a fence on your left. Go through another field, leaving it by a stile in the bottom left-hand corner to reach the B5032

Turn right and walk about 100 yds along the road, then turn left along the track beside 'The Lodge'. Reaching some gates the track splits. Do not go right here but forward through the gates beside a large house, soon meeting a drive beside a bungalow.

At this point you have a choice, either to complete the full walk via Ellastone or to take the shorter route. If you wish to do the shorter walk turn left along the drive and then continue from the paragraph marked ➡ *on p.97.*

Turn right along the drive, soon arriving at what is left of the old Calwich Abbey. The original abbey was founded in 1149 in this prime spot beside the River Dove — which in medieval times was an important line of communication. But the abbey was never a very strong institution. The maximum number of incumbents was about six, and in 1530, after the death of the abbot, was just one! The abbey was then converted into a mansion, later to be demolished and replaced by a new building. This in turn was demolished in the 1850s and again re-built. A further demolition in 1927 left just the stables and the servants quarters. These were converted into a farm which, now semi-derelict, is all that remains today.

Weir on the River Dove

Follow the well worn track along the Abbey grounds until the track divides. Take the right fork forward through a metal gate, pass a pond surrounded by trees on the left side, and follow the track through Calwich Park, swinging right to arrive at Lodge House gate. Go through the gate onto the B5032, turn left over a bridge and after about 100 yds go right through a stile to cross a field towards the pretty twelfth century St Peter's Church in Ellastone.

Go through the wooden gate into the old churchyard and immediately turn left behind the church. Leave the churchyard through the lichgate, go forward, then left to reach the B5032 again and turn right along this. This will bring you to the Duncombe Arms where you might like to make a break for some refreshment. It has an attractive garden at the back. You have now covered six miles.

From the pub go north-east along the B5032 to return to Lodge House and retrace your path back through Calwich Park and past the Abbey. Now stay on the drive which you joined earlier.

➡ *Continue from this point if you are doing the shorter walk.*

After passing Calwich Nurseries you will see across to the right the 'Fishing Temple', also known as 'Handel's Temple', dating from 1797. The composer Handel was a frequent visitor to the mansion and it is reputed locally that he wrote *The Messiah* in this building — to which the gentry would retire for drinks and relaxation. Handel was a friend of the French philosopher Rousseau who was a visitor to the nearby Wootton Lodge, some three miles to the north-west of Ellastone.

The track gradually ascends giving good views of the Dove to the right. Just after it starts to swing sharp left to Calwich Home Farm take the track on the right by the side of a house. This soon forks: take the left fork which brings you down to a double set of gates with stiles leading you to the River Dove near to a weir.

Ignore the snaking away of the Dove and cross the field in front of you, so making a short cut to where the river comes back on itself. Now follow the river along a reasonably well marked path.

After you come to the second weir the path soon bends away from the river although it does make another brief encounter with it before swinging left to arrive at a lane. Turn right along this, passing a trout farm and Mayfield Church, back past the terraced houses that you saw earlier. Take the narrow fenced lane on the right, go past the allotments and back over the narrow bridge and the Dove, through the mill houses and past the cotton mill. Return along the road, over the bridge, then follow the lane back past the old railway house. Turn sharp right up the steep road. You will then see the church and you are back in Clifton for your car or to return along the A515 to Ashbourne.

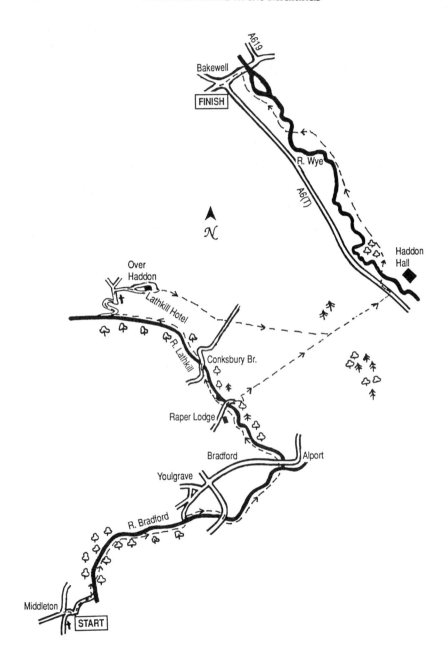

22

Derbyshire Dales — Middleton to Bakewell

by
Peter Groves

The Peak District is a fine area for a day's walking. This walk follows two dales, Bradford Dale and Lathkill Dale, then goes along the River Wye into Bakewell.

> MAPS: Landranger 119
> White Peak Leisure Map (1:25,000)
> CAR PARKING: Car parks in Bakewell. Roadside parking in Middleton.
> BUSES: Bakewell to Middleton (infrequent service). Regular service Derby and Matlock to Bakewell.
> RAILWAY STATIONS: Derby, Matlock.
> START: Middleton (GR 196632)
> FINISH: Bakewell (GR 217685)
> DISTANCE: 6 or 8 miles.

From the centre of Middleton village take the lane that goes down beside Green Farm and through fine limestone cliffs to Bradford Dale. When you reach the River Bradford note the attractive stone sheep enclosure and sheep-wash on your right.

Turn left and walk along the wooded dale which has, unfortunately, suffered in places from Dutch elm disease. You soon cross to the other side of the river and continue on the right hand side until reaching a clapper bridge which you cross. The road leads up into Youlgrave (as the locals prefer to spell it — the Ordnance Survey map gives it as Youlgreave) where there are shops, pubs and toilets. If you want to make a break here you can either go straight up the road or, if you prefer a more interesting though steeper climb, go along the path immediately to the left. This swings round to the right and brings you into the main street — turn right for shops and pubs. The Norman church with its fifteenth century tower is a prominent landmark.

Back at the river continue along the left hand bank. After crossing a road the path crosses to the right of the river. Follow this until reaching the road at Alport by a telephone box. Cross the road and take the path opposite along Lathkill Dale with the river on your right. Continue on the path until you reach a surfaced track leading down from Raper Lodge.

At this point you have a choice of routes. *For the longer route via Upper Haddon continue from the point marked* ➥ *below.* For the shorter route turn right and cross the charming stone bridge, pausing to study the fat trout which can usually be seen swimming lazily below. Over to the left you can see the trout breeding ponds.

Bradford Dale

Climb up the steep path. At the top of the hill go through the gate opposite, turn sharp right and head for a clump of trees. Go through the gate here and then straight ahead across the fields with a wall on your right. *Now continue from the point marked* ➥ *on p. 101.*

➥   If you are taking the longer route cross the surfaced track leading from Raper Lodge and take the path which continues on the other side (but you might like to first go down to the bridge to see the trout in the river).

When you reach a road turn right, cross the fine arched Conksbury Bridge and take the path left along the River Lathkill. Note the attractive weirs, built to create a series of trout pools. After a prolonged period without rain the upper part of the Lathkill dries up although the main stream continues through a natural underground channel in the underlying limestone.

When you reach a house take the road on your right and ascend steeply to Over Haddon. Passing the church you might like to go into the churchyard to see the beautiful modern sundial on the side of the church.

Turn right at the first road junction (toilets and a car park on the left) and continue through the village (where there is an excellent refreshment room). Just past a small war memorial on your left branch right down a lane which soon ascends to the Lathkill Hotel. At the sharp bend in the road here go straight forward (east) through a stile and across the field, the path going past a dead tree. At the first gate the path splits. Take the right hand path which, not being well walked, may not be very apparent. If you have a compass go forward on a magnetic bearing of 120°.

After going through a space where there was once a gate (there is a spacer stile ten yards to the left — ignore this) continue with a wall on the left over two fields bearing slightly left to reach a road. Go through the stile on the other side and cross an obscure stile over the wall ahead, midway between a water trough and the left hand corner of the field. Cross to a second water trough on the wall on your left and turn right along the track. There is an ancient tumulus on the left over the wall.

Where the track goes left through a gate continue forward and cross a stile in the next wall. Continue (bearing 120°) along an indistinct path, the wall on your left now angling away. When you reach a wall you are on the path which you would have taken if you had chosen the shorter walk. Turn left here.

➠ You will soon see Haddon Hall beside the main A6 ahead. Head for this, passing through the car park. Cross the road very carefully, turn left and walk along the A6 looking out for a stone stile in the wall (which is easy to miss!). Cross this and take the path which soon takes you across the River Wye. When reaching a surfaced track, turn right on this, then almost immediately left to gain a signed footpath which will take you to Bakewell.

After crossing a footbridge go forward with a hedge on the right, the river bending away to the left. Approaching Bakewell go through a wicket gate onto a surfaced track. Follow this and after crossing two bridges turn right along the river to reach the thirteenth century pack-horse bridge, one of the oldest in England. Leave the river here for Bakewell with its many excellent tea-shops, including the pudding shop in The Square where the famous Bakewell Puddings have been made to the original formula since 1859.

Index

An ideal walking companion

Let's Walk
by Mark Linley

Written for those who wish to join the increasing numbers who regularly escape the stresses and strains of modern life by walking in the countryside, in the hills and on the mountains, *Let's Walk*, in its sixteen chapters, gives advice and information on clothing and equipment, where to go, walking holidays, map and compass reading, wildlife, difficulties and hazards, first aid, weather, and much else.

The author, as well as being an experienced rambler, is also a skilled artist and the book is lavishly illustrated with cartoons which give a lively view of the walking scene.

"A splendid introduction to rambling. Give it to your children, in-laws, colleagues, neighbours. Or enjoy the wealth of information and 100 cartoons/sketches yourself." *The Rambler*

ISBN 1 869922 03 4. 144 pages. £4.95

Available from booksellers or, in case of difficulty, direct from the publishers. Please send remittance plus £1.00 for postage and packing.
Meridian Books
40 Hadzor Road, Oldbury, Warley, West Midlands B68 9LA